My
Video Chat
for Seniors

Michael Miller

My Video Chat for Seniors

Copyright © 2021 by Pearson Education, Inc.

Trademarks

Warning and Disclaimer

Special Sales

For information about buying this title in bulk quantities, or for special sales opportunities (which may include electronic versions; custom cover designs; and content particular to your business, training goals, marketing focus, or branding interests), please contact our corporate sales department at corpsales@pearsoned.com or (800) 382-3419.

For government sales inquiries, please contact governmentsales@pearsoned.com.

For questions about sales outside the United States, please contact intlcs@pearson.com.

Editor-in-Chief
Brett Bartow

Executive Editor
Laura Norman

Marketing
Stephane Nakib

Director, AARP Books
Jodi Lipson

Director, AARP Technology Strategy Integration
Michael Phillips

Editorial Services
The Wordsmithery LLC

Managing Editor
Sandra Schroeder

Senior Project Editor
Lori Lyons

Technical Editor
Brad Miser

Indexer
Cheryl J. Lenser

Proofreader
Sarah Kearns

Editorial Assistant
Cindy Teeters

Designer
Chuti Prasertsith

Compositor
Bronkella Publishing

Graphics
TJ Graham Art

Contents at a Glance

Table of Contents

CV 02.03.2021 1217

12 Tips and Tricks for Better Video Chats   195

15 Staying Safe While Video Chatting   253

About the Author

Michael Miller, a popular and prolific writer of more than 200 nonfiction books, is known for his ability to explain complex topics to everyday readers. He writes about a variety of topics, including technology, business, and music. His best-selling books for Que include *My iPad for Seniors*, *My TV for Seniors*, *My Windows 10 Computer for Seniors*, *My Facebook for Seniors*, *My Social Media for Seniors*, *My Internet for Seniors*, and *Computer Basics: Absolute Beginner's Guide*. Worldwide, his books have sold more than 1.5 million copies.

Find out more at the author's website: www.millerwriter.com

Follow the author on Twitter: molehillgroup

Dedication

To all the schoolkids who had to adapt to Zoom and distance learning during the COVID-19 crisis, including my grandchildren Alethia, Collin, Hayley, Jackson, Judah, and Lael.

Acknowledgments

Thanks to all the folks at Que/Pearson who helped make this book a reality, including but not limited to Laura Norman, Charlotte Kughen, Lori Lyons, Tricia Bronkella, Cheryl Lenser, Tammy Graham, and Sarah Kearns. Thanks also to technical editor Brad Miser, who verified all the technical details in the book and offered many useful suggestions. Special thanks to Jodi Lipson and Michael Phillips at AARP for recognizing the opportunity for this book, offering many good content ideas, and quickly and painstakingly reviewing the manuscript.

Finally, thanks to all my family members who willingly (or not) agreed to help out with all the many screenshots in this book. I couldn't have done it without you!

About AARP

AARP is a nonprofit, nonpartisan organization, with a membership of nearly 38 million, that helps people turn their goals and dreams into *real possibilities*™, strengthens communities, and fights for the issues that matter most to families such as healthcare, employment and income security, retirement planning, affordable utilities, and protection from financial abuse. Learn more at aarp.org.

We Want to Hear from You!

As the reader of this book, *you* are our most important critic and commentator. We value your opinion and want to know what we're doing right, what we could do better, what areas you'd like to see us publish in, and any other words of wisdom you're willing to pass our way.

You can email or write to let us know what you did or didn't like about this book—as well as what we can do to make our books better.

Please note that we cannot help you with technical problems related to the topic of this book.

When you write, please be sure to include this book's title and author, as well as your name, email address, and phone number. We will carefully review your comments and share them with the author and editors who worked on the book.

Email: community@informit.com

Reader Services

Register your copy of *My Video Chat for Seniors* at informit.com for convenient access to downloads, updates, and corrections as they become available. To start the registration process, go to www.informit.com/register and log in or create an account.* Enter the product ISBN, 9780137381258, and click Submit.

*Be sure to check the box that you would like to hear from us in order to receive exclusive discounts on future editions of this product.

Figure Credits

Chapter	Figure	Page	Credit
Cover			Marish/Shutterstock
			Svetolk/Shutterstock
1	FIGCO-01	2	milkos/123RF
1	UNFIG01-01	4	stockwars/Shutterstock
1	UNFIG01-02	9	Melinda Nagy/Shutterstock
2	UNFIG02-01B	16	rawpixel/123RF
2	UNFIG02-01C	16	Oleg Doroshenko/123RF
2	UNFIG02-01D	16	Natalia Gavrilova/123RF
2	UNFIG02-01E	16	9nong/123RF
3	FIGCO-03B	38	rawpixel/123RF
3	FIGCO-03C	38	Oleg Doroshenko/123RF
3	FIGCO-03D	38	Natalia Gavrilova/123RF
3	FIGCO-03E	38	9nong/123RF
3	UNFIG-02B	42	rawpixel/123RF
3	UNFIG-06B	46	Natalia Gavrilova/123RF
3	UNFIG-18B	53	9nong/123RF
3	UNFIG-21B	55	Oleg Doroshenko/123RF
3	UNFIG-23B	56	rawpixel/123RF
3	UNFIG-23C	56	Oleg Doroshenko/123RF
3	UNFIG-23D	56	Natalia Gavrilova/123RF
3	UNFIG-23E	56	9nong/123RF
3	UNFIG-24B	56	rawpixel/123RF
3	UNFIG-24C	56	milkos/123RF
3	UNFIG-25B	57	9nong/123RF
3	UNFIG-28B	58	rawpixel/123RF
3	UNFIG-29B	59	rawpixel/123RF
3	UNFIG-29C	59	milkos/123RF
5	FIGCO-05B	94	Natalia Gavrilova/123RF
6	FIGCO-06B	104	Oleg Doroshenko/123RF
6	UNFIG06-20B	115	milkos/123RF
7	FIGCO-07A	118	9nong/123RF
7	FIGCO-07B	118	rawpixel/123RF
7	UNFIG07-21	130	rawpixel/123RF

Chapter	Figure	Page	Credit
10	FIGCO-10B	160	Oleg Doroshenko/123RF
10	FIGCO-10C	160	milkos/123RF
10	FIGCO-10D	160	9nong/123RF
10	UNFIG10-02B	163	milkos/123RF
10	UNFIG10-12B	166	Oleg Doroshenko/123RF
10	UNFIG10-12C	166	milkos/123RF
10	UNFIG10-12D	166	9nong/123RF
12	FIGCO-12	194	fizkes/Shutterstock
13	FIGCO-13	216	Agenturfotografin/Shutterstock
13	UNFIG13-02	221	FoodAndPhoto/Shutterstock
13	UNFIG13-05	226	photowarehouse/123RF
14	FIGCO-14	238	Twinsterphoto/Shutterstock
15	FIGCO-15	252	milkos/123RF
15	UNFIG15-01	265	Lio Putra/123RF

In this chapter, you learn the basics of video chatting.

→ What Video Chat Is—and How It Works
→ How and Why People Use Video Chat
→ Video Chatting on Different Devices

1

Understanding Video Chat: What It Is and How It's Keeping Us Connected

Video chat was popular before 2020, but the coronavirus pandemic made it almost mandatory in many households. In an era when many of us were forced to quarantine at home, we found new ways to keep in touch with our family and friends and maintain some of our regular social activities. The solution, in many cases, was to use video chat technology to connect one on one and in groups using our computers, tablets, or phones. With video chatting, we get to talk to other people face to face—no matter where we or they live, work, or travel.

What Video Chat Is—and How It Works

When the COVID-19 lockdown struck, many of our activities had to go remote: doctor's appointments, school classrooms, family holidays, worship services, and more. Even though video chatting is relatively new to many people—35 percent of people using it now never used it before the pandemic—it's quickly become a regular thing. And I expect most people will continue using it long after the pandemic is over.

What Video Chat Is

What, exactly, is video chat? It's the modern equivalent of the futuristic "video-phone" that George and Jane Jetson used in their 1962–63 cartoon, or the "picturephone" that Bell Labs promised us back in the early 1960s. In essence, video chat lets you talk to one or more other people, with both audio and video, using your computer or mobile device.

You see the person or people you're chatting with on the screen of your device, and they see you on their screen, in real time. One on one, you typically see the other person in the main part of the screen and see yourself in a smaller thumbnail window in the corner. In a group chat, you may see all the participants in their own onscreen boxes, like those squares on *The Brady Bunch*.

What's in a Name?

Some folks call video chat "video calling," others call it "video conferencing," and still others calling it "video meeting." In this book, I call it "video chat." Whatever you call it, it's a way to talk to other people face-to-face over the Internet.

How Video Chat Works

A video chat starts when the parties log onto a call or when one of the parties contacts another via a phone number or email address, and the other picks up. The video chat stays live until one or the other party disconnects or, for some platforms, when the host closes the meeting or the meeting time expires.

This takes place on a specific video chat platform used by all the participants in the chat. The most popular platforms among consumers today are Apple FaceTime, Facebook Messenger, Google Duo, Google Meet, Microsoft Teams, Skype, WhatsApp, and Zoom. All participants must be on the same platform. The various platforms don't connect to each other; you have to choose the platform you want to use and make sure the people you want to talk to are connected to that platform. In other words, all the parties would need to have Facetime or Skype or Zoom to chat with each other.

All these chat platforms run on a variety of different devices and platforms— Chromebook, Mac, and Windows computers, as well as Android and iOS (Apple) phones and tablets. There are also so-called "smart displays"—the Amazon Echo Show, Facebook Portal, and Google Nest Hub Max—that facilitate video chatting on their built-in displays. Every product's platform is proprietary.

How and Why People Use Video Chat

Video chat isn't a new technology; it's been around for home use, in one form or another, for more than two decades. It's only in recent years that video chat has gained in popularity, however, as more and more people work remotely or want to stay in touch with distant family and friends.

How, exactly, do people use video chat today? Let us count the reasons.

Chatting with Friends and Family

Probably the most common reason people use video chat is to stay in touch with friends and family. Maybe your children or grandchildren live in another state. Maybe they live down the street but circumstances prevent you from visiting in person. Maybe you want to chat with all of your siblings at once, but they're spread across the country. Maybe it's time to catch up with an old friend who lives someplace else.

During the COVID-19 crisis, my wife and I both had the virus, and we had to quarantine away from our grandkids, even though they all live within a mile of our house. There's no way a video call replaces a long hug, but it was still nice to see them every night on our iPad.

Now that we're well, video chat is still great to see how things are going—or for story time. We use video chat to read stories to one of our younger grandchildren. And our third-grade granddaughter, who has become quite the avid reader, likes to call us and read to us from her books.

Meeting in Groups

As I've mentioned, video chat can be a one-on-one or group thing. There are lots of formerly in-person groups that transitioned to virtual meetings during the COVID-19 crisis. Some of them are likely to remain virtual because members don't have to be physically nearby to meet with video chat.

I know of people using video chat for their book clubs, worship services and Bible study, neighborhood association meetings, and even school board meetings. A lot of students do their study groups via video chat. Some people meet via video chat to play card games. In fact, just about anything you can do in a physical group, you can do online in a video chat.

Holding Business Meetings

Video chat has long been used by businesses to conduct face-to-face meeting with employees without everyone being in the same room. Small businesses might hold video chats with a half-dozen key employees; large businesses might hold video meetings with hundreds of participants. Many businesspeople use video chat to collaborate on team projects. Some use video chat to meet with clients or vendors.

Video chat is particularly useful for companies and organizations with multiple offices in different locations and with employees who work remotely. With video chat, a business "team" can consist of members located all around the country, or even in different countries.

Having Virtual Parties and Celebrations

During the COVID-19 crisis, it just wasn't safe to hold large parties and celebrations. Fortunately, people quickly learned how to move their gathering online via video chat. Instead of in-person birthday parties, with everybody in the same room, people started holding virtual parties, with participants in their own homes but onscreen in their own little section of the grid.

All sorts of parties and celebrations are now being conducted via video chat—birthday parties, graduation parties, anniversary parties, b'nai mitzvahs, and even big neighborhood or family holiday parties. I know of several people who've held virtual weddings and wedding receptions, which makes it easier for out-of-state guests to attend. A colleague attended a few funerals and celebrations of life online so that friends and family from all across the country could safely attend.

Engaging in Distance Learning

When the nation's schools were forced to close during the COVID-19 crisis, children from preschool through college were suddenly forced into distance learning. There are many aspects to distance learning, but one of them is communicating with teachers and other students via video chat. Zoom, especially, got a big uptick from schools moving to distance learning; Zoom classes suddenly became a thing.

Distance learning isn't just for kids, however. Students of all ages are taking classes via video chat. We're talking yoga and Pilates classes, cooking classes, crafts classes, even auto repair classes. I have several musician friends who are giving guitar and piano lessons via video chat. Online classes via video chat have become part of the norm.

Participating in Telehealth Appointments

The COVID-19 crisis accelerated the embrace of what we now call telehealth or telemedicine, where you meet with your medical professional via video chat. Most telehealth is done via proprietary video chat platforms to ensure patient privacy; you install the necessary app on your phone or log in to a secure website to have your visit—though if you need lab tests, a flu shot, or an X-ray, you will need to go into an office. I've been seeing my doctors remotely for the better part of a year now, and it works fine.

Providing Remote Caregiving

Video chat has also changed the way some people provide caregiving to their clients or loved ones. When in-person visits are impractical, caregivers can check in via video chat—often using dedicated video chat devices, such as the Amazon Echo Show or Facebook Portal. With video chat, you can watch your family members or clients from wherever you are via your phone or computer so you can offer help and support remotely.

And More...

The uses of video chat are virtually endless. People are using video chat for dog training, online talent shows, training for sports teams, meditation, children's playdates, real estate showings, karaoke, dating, dance parties, dinner parties, and even movie parties (where people in different locations watch and dish on the same film in real time). Many performers and venues are also streaming online plays and concerts via video chat.

In short, how you use video chat is limited only by your imagination—and the imagination of others.

>>>*Go Further*
PASSIVE AND ACTIVE VIDEO CHATTING

There are two ways to video chat—actively and passively. In an active video chat, all parties can both watch and participate. In a passive video chat, there is typically one or more presenters, and everybody else just watches. Webinars and lectures are passive chats, sometimes referred to as "live streaming." One-on-one and most small group meetings are active chats.

Video Chatting on Different Devices

You can video chat using your laptop, desktop computer, smartphone, or tablet. The experience is somewhat different depending on your device.

Video Chat on a Computer

To chat with your computer, it has to have a built-in or external webcam. From there, it's a matter of adjusting the camera so that it's pointing at your smiling face and then launching the video chat platform of choice.

On either your laptop or desktop computer, you'll probably access video chat through the platform's website using your web browser. Some chat platforms have their own computer software you need to install and use. Whether you're chatting through a chat program or your web browser, the experience should be similar.

The nice thing about video chatting on a computer is that, if you'd like, you can multitask while you're chatting. You can keep the chat open in one browser window while you open other windows to browse social media, check your email, or work in Microsoft Word.

You can also use your computer's mouse and keyboard to control various functions of the video chat. For example, on most video chat platforms, all it takes is a click of the mouse or a press of a specific keyboard shortcut to mute your microphone or switch to a different onscreen view. You can also easily use your keyboard to type text messages to other participants during a video chat.

Another benefit to using your computer for video chat is that your screen is larger than your phone's or tablet's. This may not matter if you're chatting one-on-one with a friend or family member, but when you're participating in a group chat with a number of other people, the thumbnail for each person can get pretty tiny on a smaller phone or tablet screen. On a larger computer display, you can better see who you're talking with.

>>>Go Further

WHAT YOU NEED

To video chat, you need a device with a microphone, speaker, display (screen or monitor), and a camera. Today's smartphones and tablets have all four of these things built in, as do laptop computers of various flavors—Chromebooks, Macs, and Windows. Desktop computers, however, are a different matter.

Some all-in-one desktops have built-in cameras and microphones, but most traditional desktops don't. If your computer doesn't have a built-in camera and microphone, you can purchase and connect an external *webcam*—a device with a camera and microphone that sits on top of your monitor. Webcams start at about $30 and are manufactured and sold by Aluratek, AUKEY, Logitech, and other companies. (Learn more about webcams in Chapter 13, "Enhancing Your Video Chats with Add-Ons and Accessories.")

Video Chat on a Tablet

Video chatting on an iPad or other tablet is much the same as chatting on a computer, except with a smaller screen and without a mouse and keyboard. When you want to access the functions of a chat platform (muting, changing views, and so forth), you have to reach over and tap the screen with your finger, which can look a little weird to the people you're chatting with.

The other thing you have to deal with when chatting on a tablet is positioning the tablet so that the camera gets a good view of you. Many tablet cases fold up or over to let you rest the tablet on a desk or other flat surface, typically at a slight angle. If you don't have such a case, you'll have to hold the tablet throughout the whole chat.

Tablet and Phone Stands

Learn more about desktop stands for tablets and phones in Chapter 13.

Video Chat on a Mobile Phone

When video chatting on your phone, you have a much smaller screen to work with, which can make seeing individuals on group chats difficult. If you don't have a stand, you may also have to hold the phone throughout the entire chat, which can get tiring.

Now, if you're doing a short one-on-one video chat, using your phone is probably fine. In fact, using your phone may be easier if you are in the car, taking a walk, or moving about.

Some video chat platforms are optimized for mobile phone use—and some, like WhatsApp, work only on mobile phones. It really depends on the type of chatting you'll be doing and whether you have a more appropriate device available.

Video Chat on a Smart Display

There is a new category of devices, called *smart displays*, that are designed at least in part for video chatting. These include the Amazon Echo Show, Facebook Portal, and Google Nest Hub Max, all of which are available in various screen sizes. These smart displays include a screen, microphone, camera, and speaker and a voice interface that easily responds to your commands ("Alexa, call Mom")—everything you need for video chatting and nothing more.

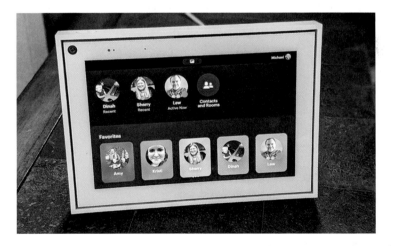

The Facebook Portal Mini smart display with dedicated video chatting

The advantage of using a dedicated device for video chatting is that it's extremely easy to set up and use. They're also more affordable than buying a new computer or smartphone. Prices on these devices run from $100 to $300.

If you have a family member or friend who isn't tech-savvy, you might want to set that person up with one of these smart display devices. That way, when it's time to chat, the person can easily answer and participate.

Smart Displays

Learn more about these smart displays in Chapter 11, "Video Chatting with Facebook Portal, Amazon Echo Show, and Google Nest Hub Max."

>>>Go Further
VIDEO CHAT IN THE COVID AGE

Video chatting got a huge boost when the COVID-19 crisis forced tens of millions of people inside their homes. What was once a theoretical future full of video meetings, distance learning, and telehealth visits suddenly became a reality of daily Skype calls and Zoom meetings. The world changed overnight, and with it the world of video chatting.

The sudden and somewhat-forced embrace of video chat during COVID was the only way an isolated populace could deal with the social distancing required to fight the global pandemic. Not everybody liked spending so much time on video chats, but it was literally the only way we could keep in touch with one another.

In a way, we were fortunate that the pandemic happened when it did. If the crisis had happened just a few short years earlier, when fewer of us had high-speed Internet connections, whole-house Wi-Fi, and a bevy of connected devices within reach, video chat wouldn't have been a viable option, and we all would have been left by ourselves in the virtual cold. Because of the advances in Internet-based technology, many of us were fortunate to be able to almost immediately shift from in-person meetings to online ones.

The COVID-19 crisis also helped us realize that some meetings don't need to be held face to face. When all the unpleasantness has subsided, we'll likely see a permanent decrease in business travel, conferences and seminars, and some in-person gatherings, which have all been at least partially replaced by video chat.

In other words, video chat is here to stay.

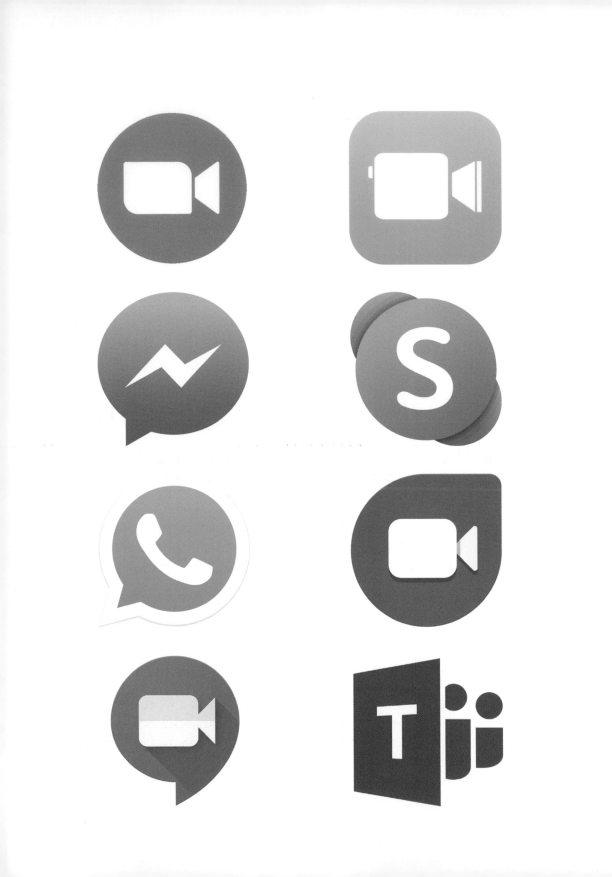

Comparing Video Chat Platforms

All the video chat platforms discussed in this book do pretty much the same thing in pretty much the same fashion—although there are some differences between them. The question, then, is which video chat platform should you use—under which circumstances.

Read on to learn about the major video chat platforms: their main features, what devices they work on, their pros, and their cons. It'll help you choose which video chat platforms to use—and when.

Introducing the Major Video Chat Platforms

Which video chat platform you use when depends on the device you use, the number of people you want to chat with, how long you want to talk, and more. This section covers eight video chat platforms, all free and popular with individual users.

Zoom

Zoom is the most popular video chat platform today, used by about two-thirds of all people doing video chatting. Zoom started out targeting large businesses but gained popularity among individuals, schools, houses of worship, and other organizations with the onset of the COVID-19 pandemic. Today people use Zoom to connect with friends and family, hold small group meetings, do distance learning, celebrate milestones such as birthdays and anniversaries, conduct business meetings, and much more.

A Zoom meeting on an iPad

One reason Zoom became so popular is because it's fully cross-platform. That means anyone on any device—Android or iOS (Apple) phone or tablet, or Chromebook, Mac, or Windows computer—can use Zoom, as long as the device is connected to the Internet.

Another factor is that Zoom is extremely easy to use. You simply set up an account and download the app. Then the organizer, or host, enters the phone number or email addresses of the invited participants, each of whom receives a text message or email with a link. To join the meeting, just click the link. The first time you use Zoom, you're prompted to install the Zoom app (Zoom calls it the "Zoom client," and it's free), but on subsequent uses, the app should launch automatically. The meeting opens with all participants appearing in their own little box in the onscreen grid.

Zoom is also popular because you can share files or content so everyone can view and collaborate in real time. With the free version of Zoom, a meeting can hold up to 100 participants for 40 minutes. Learn more at www.zoom.us.

Zoom

Learn more about Zoom in Chapter 3, "Using Zoom," and Chapter 4, "Getting More Out of Zoom."

Apple FaceTime

If you have an iPhone or iPad, you've probably used FaceTime video chat. Chatting with FaceTime is as easy as making a phone call. FaceTime also works on Mac computers, although it's not available for Android phones or tablets or for Windows computers.

Group FaceTime on an iPad

Apple, iOS, and iPadOS

Apple's iPhones run an operating system known as iOS. Apple's iPads run a similar operating system called iPadOS. In this book and elsewhere, both iPhones and iPads are often referred to as iOS devices.

If you have an Apple device, FaceTime shows up as a calling feature and taps directly into your device's contacts. With the tap of an onscreen button, you can initiate or answer a video call.

If you want to hold a group video chat, you use a feature that Apple calls Group FaceTime. This lets you hold chats with up to 32 participants with no time limits.

FaceTime is included for free with all Apple computers and devices, no additional installation necessary.

FaceTime

Learn more about FaceTime in Chapter 5, "Using FaceTime."

Facebook Messenger

Facebook Messenger is a messaging and video chat app from the Facebook social network. It's available to all Facebook members on all devices (Android and iOS phones and tablets, as well as Chromebook, Mac, and Windows computers). It is only available to people who are Facebook members.

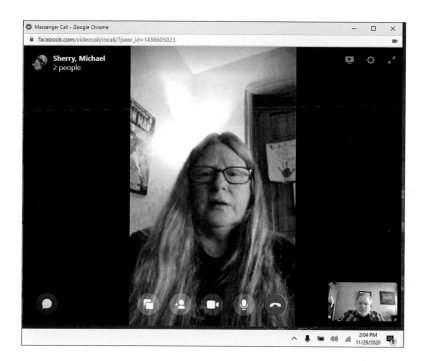

Facebook Messenger on a computer

On a computer, you use Facebook Messenger from the Facebook website, in any web browser. On phones and tablets, you download the Messenger app separately from the Facebook app or use your phone's web browser. (Facebook also makes separate Facebook Portal devices that enable Messenger voice and video calls through a smart display or, in the case of the Portal TV device, your TV.)

Messenger lets Facebook users participate in audio and video calls with their Facebook friends. By default, all calls are person to person, although Facebook offers Messenger Rooms for group chat. A Room can have up to 50 participants; you can even invite people who don't have Facebook accounts to a Room. There is no time limit on Messenger video chats.

Because of how easy it is to use—and how many people use Facebook every day—Facebook Messenger is increasing in popularity, especially among older users. Learn more at www.messenger.com.

Facebook Messenger

Learn more about Facebook Messenger in Chapter 6, "Using Facebook Messenger."

Skype

Skype was one of the first video chat platforms. Like Zoom, it's available across most major platforms—Android and iOS phones and tablets, as well as Mac and Windows computers (but not Chromebooks). I have an Android phone, and I use Skype almost daily to chat with one of my granddaughters who has an Apple iPhone.

Skype on an Android phone

Microsoft, Skype, and Teams

Skype is owned by Microsoft, which also offers the newer Microsoft Teams chat platform discussed later in this chapter. Microsoft has transitioned all Skype business users to the Teams platform but maintains the Skype platform for consumer users.

Like all the other services discussed here, Skype video chats are completely free. Learn more at www.skype.com.

Skype

Learn more about Skype in Chapter 7, "Using Skype."

WhatsApp

WhatsApp is a mobile-based messaging and video chat platform that is extremely popular among school-aged kids but is also gaining popularity among more mature users. It's actually more popular outside the United States, with a huge following in Latin America, India, and parts of Asia and Europe. The app is available for both Android and iOS devices.

The WhatsApp app on an Android phone

WhatsApp started out as a messaging platform for younger users and still is used by many to send text messages and photos to friends. (It includes lots of stickers and emoji that the kids seem to like.) The platform has added voice and video chat, as well, which makes it a popular choice, especially for those already using it for texting.

Know, however, that when it comes to voice and video chatting, WhatsApp is strictly for mobile phone users. You can voice and video chat on Android and iOS devices but not on the web-based version of the service, which is limited solely to text messages.

By default, WhatsApp video chats are one to one. You can, however, add up to eight total participants to a group video call with no time restrictions. If you want to include even more participants, you can shift from WhatsApp to Messenger Rooms in the Facebook Messenger app. (WhatsApp is owned by Facebook and shares the Messenger Rooms technology.)

WhatsApp is a free service, like all the other video chat platforms discussed here. Learn more at www.whatsapp.com.

WhatsApp

Learn more about WhatsApp in Chapter 8, "Using WhatsApp."

Google Duo

Google Duo is a newer video chat platform from Google, designed to compete with Apple FaceTime for both iPhone and Android smartphone use. You'll find Google Duo preinstalled on many Android phones (including Google's line of Pixel phones). You can also download the Duo app for free from the Google Play Store for Android devices or Apple's App Store for iPhones and iPads. There's also a web version available, so you can use it on your Chromebook, Mac, or Windows computer.

Google Duo on an Android phone

Duo is primarily designed for one-on-one video calls (and in the Android and iOS apps is integrated with your phone's calling app). You can, however, set up group video chats with up to 32 participants with no time limits. Google Duo is free, although you need a Google account to use it. Learn more at duo.google.com.

Google Duo and Google Meet

Learn more about Google Duo and Google Meet in Chapter 9, "Using Google Duo and Meet."

Google Meet

Also from Google is Google Meet. Unlike Duo, Google Meet is designed for larger video meetings of up to 100 participants for up to 60 minutes.

Google Meet on a Windows computer

Google Meet was originally designed for secure business meetings. During the early weeks of the COVID-19 crisis, however, Google reengineered it to be more consumer friendly (and to compete more directly with Zoom). Today, Google Meet is free for consumers to use; all you need is a Google account.

Google Meet is available for all devices and platforms, including Android, iOS, Mac, Windows, and Chrome OS. Google also offers paid accounts with additional features, including no 60-minute time limit on chats.

Learn more at meet.google.com.

Microsoft Teams

The final video chat platform in our sights is Microsoft Teams. Teams is actually a collaboration platform targeted at businesses as part of the Microsoft 365 offering.

Microsoft Teams on a Windows computer

The business version of Microsoft Teams includes text messaging, voice and video calling, video conferencing, and file sharing between Microsoft's Office apps; the cost is a minimum of $5 per user per month. There is also a free version of Microsoft Teams designed for consumers that focuses on messaging and audio and video chat.

This free version of Microsoft Teams includes one-on-one and group voice and video chats. It's available on all platforms, including Android and iOS as well as via web browser on Windows, Mac, and Chromebook computers. Group video chats can have up to 250 participants and last up to 24 hours, making Teams a good choice for all-day meetings or chats. Learn more at www.microsoft.com/microsoft-365/microsoft-teams/group-chat-software.

Microsoft Teams

Learn more about Microsoft Teams in Chapter 10, "Using Microsoft Teams."

>>>*Go Further*

OTHER VIDEO CHAT PLATFORMS

The eight video chat platforms discussed in this chapter are the most popular among home users, but they're not the only platforms vying for eyeballs. There are a number of video chat platforms targeted at the business or enterprise market that have millions of individual users. These platforms typically offer more functionality than mere video conferencing, including enhanced security, real-time collaboration and file sharing, and integration with Microsoft Office and other apps.

Among the most popular of these enterprise-level video communications platforms are

- BlueJeans (www.bluejeans.com)
- Cisco Webex (www.webex.com)
- GoToMeeting (www.gotomeeting.com)
- Wickr (www.wickr.com)

As noted, these platforms are not designed for casual consumer use and have few home users.

Evaluating the Major Video Chat Platforms

What are the differences between all these video chat platforms and how do they compare? Refer to Table 2.1 for a breakdown of the details of each of the major video chat platforms.

Table 2.1   Features of Major Video Chat Platforms

Chat Platform	Consumer Plans	Operating Systems/ Devices	Max Number of Users	Time Limits	Pros	Cons
Apple FaceTime	Free	iOS, Mac	32	Unlimited	Easy to use, integrated into Apple devices.	Only for users of Apple devices.
Facebook Messenger	Free	All (Android, ChromeOS, iOS, Mac, Windows)	8 (50 in Messenger Rooms)	Unlimited	Easy to call Facebook "friends," works with Facebook Portal devices.	Only for Facebook users, clunky interface, difficult to create and share "rooms," some privacy issues.
Google Duo	Free	All (Android, ChromeOS, iOS, Mac, Windows)	32	Unlimited	Easy to use, especially for Android phone users.	Users must have Google accounts.
Google Meet	Free	All (Android, ChromeOS, iOS, Mac, Windows)	100	60 minutes	Cross-platform.	Users must have Google accounts, limit on meeting length.
Microsoft Teams	Free	All (Android, ChromeOS, iOS, Mac, Windows)	250	24 hours	Largest number of participants, all-day meeting length.	Business-focused design may not be as user-friendly as other platforms.

Chat Platform	Consumer Plans	Operating Systems/ Devices	Max Number of Users	Time Limits	Pros	Cons
Skype	Free	Android, iOS, Mac, Windows	100	4 hours per call, 10 hours per day, 100 hours per month.	Cross-platform across most devices, good for group meetings.	Not available for Chromebook. Looks less modern than newer platforms.
WhatsApp	Free	Android, iOS	8	Unlimited	Primarily for smartphone users, integrates with Facebook Messenger Rooms for large group chats.	For smartphones only.
Zoom	Free	All (Android, ChromeOS, iOS, Mac, Windows)	100	40 minutes	Cross-platform across any device, easy to use, easy to share your screen.	Chats limited to 40 minutes, not able to directly call someone (must send a link).

>>>Go Further

WHICH PLATFORM IS THE MOST POPULAR?

When it comes to video chat platforms, which are the most popular? It depends on who's chatting.

Among users of all ages, Zoom is the number one platform, with 66% of the total. FaceTime is number two with 48%, followed by Facebook Messenger (31%), Skype (27%), Google Hangouts/Duo/Meet (22%), WhatsApp (19%), Microsoft Teams (17%), and other (7%), according to a survey from research firm Ipsos.

For users aged 55+, it breaks down this way:

- Zoom, 66%

- FaceTime, 43%

- Skype, 26%

- Facebook Messenger, 20%

- WhatsApp, 17%

- Microsoft Teams, 16%

- Google Hangouts/Duo/Meet, 13%

- Other, 10%

The numbers total more than 100% because many people use more than one platform.

The survey also asked why people use video chat. People aged 55+ said they use video chat for:

- Visiting with family and/or friends (72%)

- Work (33%)

- Telehealth (8%)

- Education (7%)

- Exercise (7%)

Only 1% of people in this age group said they used video chat for dating.

Which Video Chat Platform(s) Should You Use?

With all the video chat platforms available, which should you choose for yourself? Well, there's no simple answer to that because each platform has strengths and weaknesses.

You'll probably end up using more than one video chat platform, depending on your needs and who you're communicating with. Each platform has its strengths and weaknesses. Table 2.2 shows my take on which platform is best suited for what.

Table 2.2 Best Video Chat Platforms for Specific Uses

Best For	Facebook Messenger	FaceTime	Google Duo	Google Meet	Microsoft Teams	Skype	WhatsApp	Zoom
One-on-One Chats	✓	✓	✓			✓	✓	
Group Chats	✓ (Messenger Rooms)			✓		✓		✓
Business Meetings				✓	✓			✓
Live Streaming Large Meetings and Webinars				✓	✓			✓
Apple Users		✓						
Facebook Users	✓							
Video Chatting on Your Phone	✓	✓	✓				✓	

Best for One-on-One Chats

- Facebook Messenger (Facebook users only)
- FaceTime (Apple devices only)
- Google Duo
- Skype
- WhatsApp

When it comes to one-on-one video chats, you want a simple solution—and fancy group chat features don't matter much. For this scenario, if you and the person you're chatting with have Apple devices, consider FaceTime; if you're both on Facebook, go with Facebook Messenger; and for cross-platform use, go with Google Duo or Skype. WhatsApp is another option, if you and the other person you're chatting with both use it.

Best for Group Chats

- Facebook Messenger Rooms
- Google Meet
- Skype
- Zoom

For group chats, you need a solution that is cross-platform because it's likely that people in the group will be using all manner of devices—some iPhones, some Android phones, some iPads, some Windows computers, and some Mac computers. You also need a platform that's easy for everybody to use.

For all these reasons, the number one choice for small or large group chats is Zoom. It's fully cross-platform, so nobody is excluded. You can set up a chat with the press of a button, and any participant can join just by clicking a link in an email or text message. Zoom is also very versatile in operation, with multiple display options, virtual backgrounds, screensharing, and other advanced options—if you need them. You can have up to 100 participants per meeting, and the 40-minute meeting limit is not that restricting.

There are three good alternatives to Zoom for small and medium-sized group chats: Facebook Messenger Rooms, Google Meet, and Skype. All three are just about as easy to use and make it easy to create meetings and invite participants. They are also all cross-platform.

Best for Business Meetings

- Google Meet
- Microsoft Teams
- Zoom

Zoom is also the number-one choice for most business meetings. The cross-platform compatibility is a necessity, and the screen sharing and display options help make meetings more functional. Zoom also lets meeting participants engage in side text chats and makes it easy to switch Zoom from interactive to presentation mode, which is good for larger meetings.

Google Meet and Microsoft Teams are two other viable platforms for business use. Google Meet is just about as easy to use as Zoom, although all participants need Google accounts. (Most people have Google or Gmail accounts already, and it's easy enough to open a new one.) Microsoft Teams isn't quite as user-friendly as Meet or Zoom but may hold appeal for some people. Like Zoom, both offer robust screen- and file-sharing functionality; Teams also is fully integrated with all Microsoft Office apps, which most businesses use.

Best for Live Large Meetings and Seminars

- Google Meet
- Microsoft Teams
- Zoom

If you're hosting a meeting or seminar with a large number of passive participants—that is, you're not looking for interactivity—then Zoom, Google Meet, or Microsoft Teams all do the job. Zoom is probably the platform of choice, just because more people are familiar with it, but any of these three platforms offer similar functionality. It's really more about putting on a live presentation than hosting a meeting where every participant gets a voice in real time, which all three of these platforms offer the tools to do.

Best for Apple Users

- FaceTime

If you and the people you want to chat with all have Apple devices—iPhones, iPads, and Macs—then for day-to-day video chatting, FaceTime can't be beat. FaceTime works super smoothly within the Apple ecosystem, to the point where anything else seems clunky. If you're in the Apple family and are just chatting (without needing to share something on your screen), use FaceTime.

Best for Android Users

- Google Duo

If you're an Android user—with a Google Pixel, Samsung Galaxy, or similar phone or tablet—you can't use FaceTime. Instead, the best video chat platform for you is Google Duo. (In fact, Duo may already be installed on your device, especially if you have a Google Pixel phone.) Google Duo integrates well with your device's built-in phone app and, as an added benefit, is cross-platform. That means that your friends and family can install and use Google Duo on their devices, even if they're not running the Android operating system.

Best for Facebook Users

- Facebook Messenger

Here's another platform-specific recommendation. If you and your friends are all on Facebook—and are currently using Facebook Messenger to send individual and group text messages back and forth—then you might as well use Facebook Messenger for your video chats, too. Many people keep Facebook open practically 24/7 on their phones and computers, so using Facebook for video chatting feels like it's just another app in the operating system. Granted, Messenger might not have all the bells and whistles found on other chat platforms, but if all you need is the basics—and you're tied into the Facebook network—then Messenger may be the way to go.

Best for Video Chatting on Your Phone

- Facebook Messenger (Facebook users only)
- FaceTime (iPhones only)
- Google Duo
- WhatsApp

Some people video chat from their computers. Some people video chat from their tablets. But many, many people video chat from their ever-present smartphones. If this describes you, then Facebook Messenger (if you're talking to other Facebook users), Apple FaceTime (if you're talking only to fellow iPhone users), Google Duo, or WhatsApp is probably all you need. All these platforms offer simple and intuitive phone-based operation, which makes video chatting just about as easy as making a traditional phone call.

Which Device(s) Should You Use for Video Chat?

In addition to deciding on what video chat platform to use, you probably also have a choice of what device to use for your video chatting. Depending on your situation, you may be able to chat on your phone, your tablet, or your laptop or desktop computer. You may even have other options, such as a smart speaker with a screen or a dedicated video chat device, such as Facebook Portal. Which device should you chat with?

Best for One-on-One Chats

When it comes to one-on-one chats, convenience is key. This probably means using whatever device you're closest to at the moment. If you're working at your desk and want to chat, use your computer. If you're sitting in your car or your living room, just pull out your phone. You don't need a big screen to chat one-on-one with a family member or friend.

Best for Group Chats

Group chats, on the other hand, benefit from a device with a larger screen. If you have a half-dozen or more people displayed in little boxes, it's nice to have a bigger screen to see everyone clearly. This pretty much rules out using your phone. If it's a smaller group meeting, a tablet might suffice, but for meetings with large numbers of people, nothing beats the bigger screen of a laptop or (even better) desktop computer.

Best for Business Meetings

If you're participating in a business meeting, you may need access to documents and files on your computer during the meeting. This means using the same device for the video chat as you do for your regular work—either a laptop or desktop computer. This way you can open the video meeting in one window and the other documents you need in other windows—and even keep your email app going in the background, too.

Best for Mobility

When you're moving around, you need a device that's more mobile, which probably means your phone. A tablet might do in a pinch, but the good old smartphone is the ultimate mobile device.

Best for Picture Quality

So far, the focus has been on your end of the video chat. What about what other people see—the quality of the picture captured by the camera in the device you're using? Although there are significant variations in camera quality from device to device, here's some general advice.

It's likely that your phone or tablet will have a better camera than the one built into or connected to your laptop or desktop computer. You use your phone or tablet to take high-quality photographs and videos; you don't use your computer in the same fashion. For this reason, most newer and more expensive phones and even some tablets have very good cameras and lenses that take very good pictures, even in low light.

On the other hand, your computer's camera, whether built in to the device or an external webcam, is likely not optimized for picture quality and in many cases delivers much lower resolution than the cameras in many phones and tablets.

Put simply, you'll likely look better if you use the camera in your phone or tablet than if you use your computer's camera or a webcam.

If picture quality is important to a particular video chat or meeting, use the device with the best front-facing camera—which is probably your phone or tablet.

Best for Non-Technical Users

Many people use video chat to keep in touch with relatives who are less than comfortable with today's technology. Clicking into a Zoom meeting or answering a Skype call may seem easy to you but could be frustratingly beyond the capabilities of some less tech-savvy people.

If you want to chat with someone less technical who might not have a computer or tablet or even current smartphone, consider purchasing that person a device specifically for video chatting. There are several available.

First, there are smart displays, which are like smart speakers (like the Amazon Echo Dot) but with a screen. If you're in the Amazon ecosystem, that means the Echo Show (www.amazon.com); in the Google ecosystem, that's a Nest Hub Max (store.google.com/product/google_nest_hub_max). If you have a similar device in your home, it's extremely easy to make a video call from your device to the other one, or vice versa.

Video chatting on an Amazon Echo Show device

Video Chat Devices

Learn more about chatting with dedicated video chat devices in Chapter 11, "Video Chatting with Facebook Portal, Amazon Echo Show, and Google Nest Hub Max."

Then there's the Facebook Portal (portal.facebook.com), which is a family of devices designed specifically for video chatting over the Facebook Messenger service. Facebook offers several portals with their displays of various sizes, as well as a Portal TV unit which has a built-in camera and connects to your TV to view the video chat. The Portal TV gained popularity during the COVID-19 crisis and is especially popular among older users.

Using Zoom

Zoom is the most popular video chat platform for both home and business users. It's compatible with all devices and technology platforms, including Windows, Mac, and Chromebook computers, as well as Android and iOS (Apple) phones and tablets.

Learning All About Zoom

Zoom is used by about two-thirds of all individuals doing video chatting. It's easy to use and, for home users, it's free.

In Zoom world, a video chat is called a Zoom meeting. You can have up to 100 participants in a Zoom meeting, and each chat can last up to 40 minutes long. (Sometimes, Zoom will extend your time. Or, if you need more than 40 minutes, you can easily schedule or launch a second meeting immediately following the first one.)

Zoom Chat

Zoom doesn't call its Zoom meetings video chats. In fact, in Zoom parlance, Zoom Chat is a separate Internet-based telephone service for large enterprises. So in this book, I refer to Zoom meetings.

Zoom runs as an app on your mobile device or computer, or within a web browser on a computer. The first time you use Zoom from Zoom's website, you're prompted to download and install the app. The app is free, and you can download and install it before you start using Zoom, if you want. Alternatively, you can access Zoom from its website without installing the app on your computer.

The entire Zoom meeting takes place over the Internet, so all meeting participants must be connected to the Internet. Your Internet connection can be via Wi-Fi or Ethernet or, if you have a phone, using mobile data.

>>>*Go Further*

ZOOM FOR BUSINESS

Zoom started as a video conferencing service for businesses and continues to serve that market. Zoom for business differs from the home-based version by allowing longer meetings with more participants, cloud-based recording, user management via an admin portal, and detailed reporting.

Unlike Zoom's home version, the business version of Zoom isn't free. Zoom offers several different plans, starting at $149.90 per year and going up from there. Zoom also offers several business add-ons to its basic service, including options for audio calling, cloud storage, and larger groups.

For information on Zoom for business, go to www.zoom.us/pricing.

Using Zoom on Different Devices

The Zoom interface looks slightly different from device to device. Let's see what you can expect when you start using Zoom.

It May Look Different

The Zoom interface, placement of various controls, and even the labeling on different controls may look different on your device than what I show here because Zoom is not totally standardized across all devices; it really does look a little different depending on what device you're using. It also looks a little different the first time you use it than in subsequent uses; in addition, some things change depending on whether you're a host or a participant. Zoom also updates its apps on a regular basis, so things might change with an update. In most instances, the changes aren't major, however, and you should be able to figure them out.

Zoom on a Computer

You can launch the Zoom software manually from the Zoom website or from any meeting link you've been sent. The first screen you see is the Home screen. This screen includes four tabs, aligned across the top.

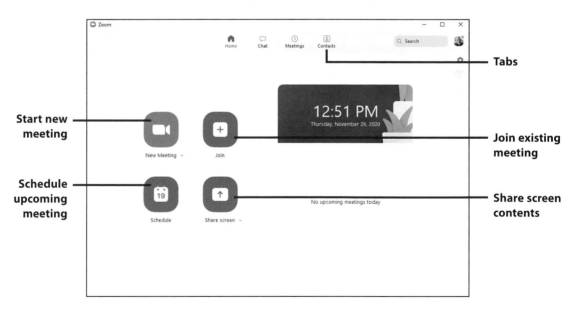

Zoom's Home screen on a Windows computer

- **Home:** This is your main screen. From here, you can launch a new meeting, join an existing meeting, schedule an upcoming meeting, or share your screen with other meeting participants.

- **Chat:** This screen lets you exchange public text messages with everyone on the meeting or private text messages with individual users.

- **Meetings:** This screen displays your personal meeting ID, as well as any meetings you've recorded.

- **Contacts:** Use this screen to manage your Zoom contacts.

When you launch or enter a meeting, you see the meeting screen. By default, the person speaking takes up the large part of the screen, while you appear in a small thumbnail window in the corner of the screen. (You can change this view, as I discuss later in this chapter.) Hover your mouse over the screen to display Zoom meeting controls.

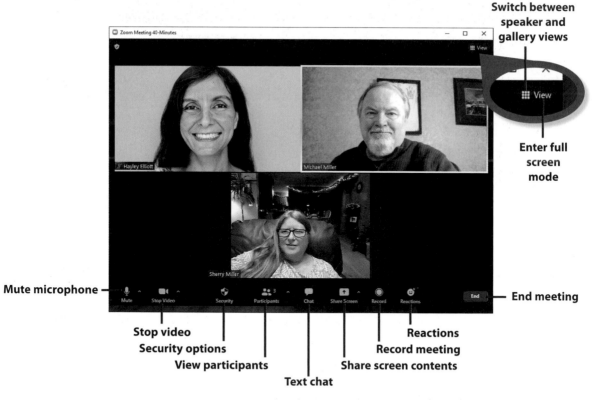

A Zoom meeting on a Windows computer showing Gallery view

Zoom on an iPad

Using Zoom on an iPad or other tablet is a lot like using it on a computer, even if the controls may be in different places than they are on your computer.

When you launch the Zoom app, the first screen you see is the Home screen. This screen includes four tabs on the left side of the screen.

Start new meeting — Join existing meeting

Schedule upcoming meeting — Share screen contents

Tabs

Zoom's Home screen on an iPad

- **Home:** From here, you can launch a new meeting, join an existing meeting, schedule an upcoming meeting, or share your screen with other meeting participants.

- **Chats:** This screen lets you exchange public text messages with everyone in the meeting or private text messages with individual users.

- **Meetings:** This screen displays your personal meeting ID.

- **Contacts:** Use this screen to manage your Zoom contacts.

When you launch or enter a meeting, you see the meeting screen. By default, the person speaking takes up the large part of the screen, while you appear in a small thumbnail window in the corner of the screen. (This is called Speaker view.) Tap the screen to display Zoom meeting controls.

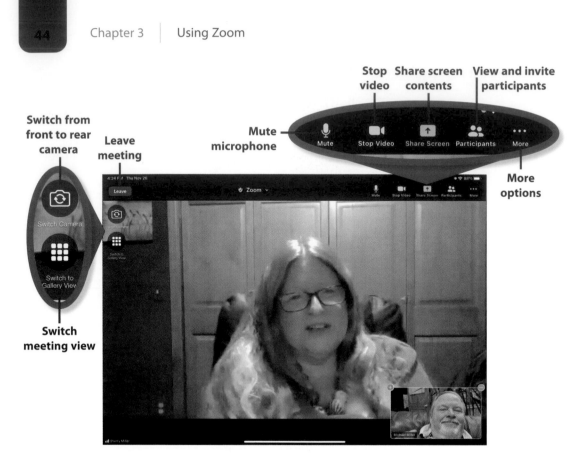

Stop video

Share screen contents

View and invite participants

Switch from front to rear camera

Leave meeting

Mute microphone

More options

Switch meeting view

A Zoom meeting on an iPad

Zoom on a Phone

Zooming on an Android phone or iPhone is a slightly different experience because of the smaller screen. Things are a little more compact.

When you launch the Zoom app, you see the Meet & Chat screen. There are four tabs along the bottom of the screen.

Join existing meeting

Start new meeting

Schedule upcoming meeting

Share screen contents

Tabs

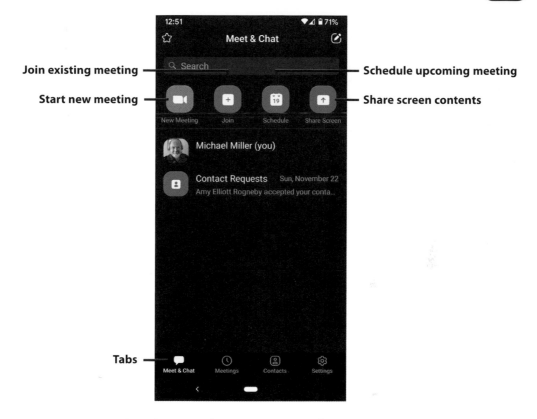

Zoom's Meet & Chat screen on an Android phone

- **Meet & Chat:** From here, you can launch a new meeting, join an existing meeting, schedule an upcoming meeting, or share your screen with other meeting participants.

- **Meetings:** This screen displays your personal meeting ID.

- **Contacts:** Use this screen to manage your Zoom contacts.

- **Settings:** Manage all Zoom settings.

When you launch or enter a meeting, you see the meeting screen. You can hold your phone vertically (portrait mode) or horizontally (landscape mode); the controls rotate accordingly. Tap to display the onscreen controls.

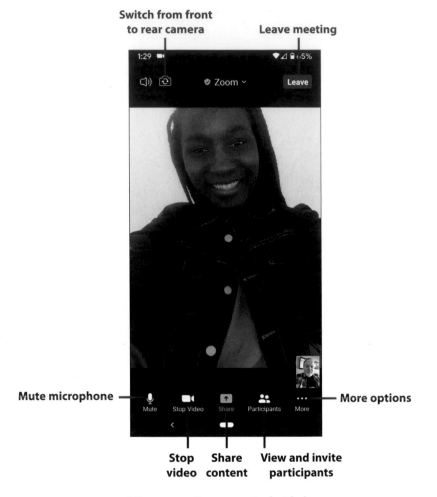

Switch from front to rear camera

Leave meeting

Mute microphone

More options

Stop video   **Share content**   **View and invite participants**

A Zoom meeting on an Android phone

Participating in a Zoom Meeting

Now that you kind of know your way around Zoom on various devices, let's move forward and talk about how to participate in a Zoom meeting.

Display Name

When you first sign up for a Zoom account, you're prompted to create your display name. Choose this name wisely because it's the name displayed to all the other participants in all the Zoom meetings you attend. Most of the time, your first and last name suffice, but if you use a nickname, you may want to enter that, instead. (To change your name when you're in a Zoom meeting, click or tap More and then select Rename.)

Accept an Email Invitation

The host of a Zoom meeting sends out invitations to all participants. This is true of chats being held immediately and those scheduled for a future time.

Invitations can be via email or text. This task explains how to join a Zoom meeting via an email invitation.

1 From within the email, click the link for the Zoom meeting.

First Meeting

If this is your very first Zoom meeting, you'll be prompted to download the Zoom app to your device and create a Zoom account. If you've already downloaded the app but not signed in, you'll be prompted to do that now. On a computer, you can also join the meeting from your web browser without downloading the app, as I discuss on the next page.

2 If you're prompted to join with or use your device's audio and/or video, do so.

3 You may be placed in a virtual waiting room until admitted by the host. This is particularly the case if you join a scheduled meeting a few minutes early or the meeting has a waiting room.

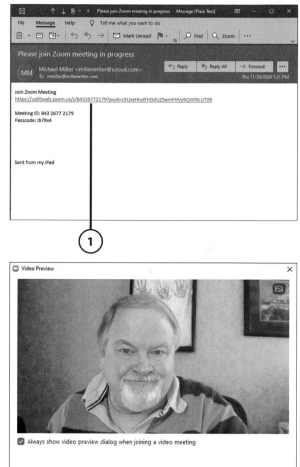

(4) Once you're admitted to the meeting, you're ready to go. (If you're further prompted to join with your device's audio or video, do so.)

(4)

Turn On Your Camera and Microphone

When you enter a Zoom meeting, your camera and microphone may be turned off, which means nobody can see or hear you. Check your camera and microphone settings and, if necessary, switch them both on.

>>>Go Further
USE ZOOM FROM A WEB BROWSER

While Zoom likes for computer users to chat via its desktop app, you can also use Zoom from within your web browser. This method has two advantages—you don't have to install any software on your computer and you don't have to create a Zoom account to join a meeting. Using Zoom via the Web is also more secure than using the desktop app.

To use Zoom from your web browser, click the link in the email invitation. A new tab opens in your web browser. Instead of clicking the (large and prominent) link to launch or install the Zoom desktop software, look for a (typically much smaller) link labeled Join from Your Browser. Click this link, and you join the meeting directly from your web browser instead of from the Zoom app.

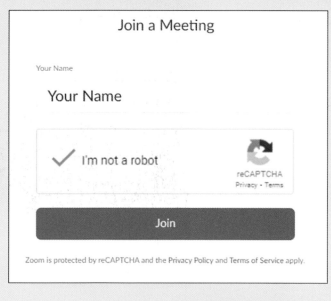

> Don't have Zoom Client installed? Download Now
>
> Having issues with Zoom Client? Join from Your Browser

Click the Join from Your Browser link.

Participating in a Zoom meeting from your computer's web browser is very similar to doing so from the Zoom desktop app. The interface and functionally is practically identical.

The big difference is that when you join a meeting from your browser, you have to enter your name manually. That's because you're joining anonymously, not from a Zoom account. Make sure you do this so everybody in the meeting knows who you are!

Join a Meeting

Your Name

Your Name

✓ I'm not a robot   reCAPTCHA
Privacy · Terms

Join

Zoom is protected by reCAPTCHA and the Privacy Policy and Terms of Service apply.

Enter your name manually to enter the meeting.

Accept a Text Invitation

Some hosts send invitations via text so that you can join the meeting directly from your phone. (You can also use the information in the text to join the meeting manually, as described in the next task.)

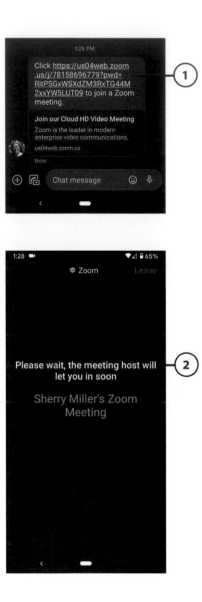

(1) From within the text, tap the link for the Zoom meeting. If you're prompted to sign in or to join with or use your phone's audio and/or video, do so.

(2) You may be placed in a virtual waiting room until admitted by the host. If so, wait for the meeting to begin.

(**3**) Once you're admitted to the meeting, you're ready to go.

Enter a Meeting Manually

Clicking or tapping a link is the easiest way to join a Zoom meeting, but it's not the only way. When you receive an invitation via email or text, that invitation should include the meeting ID and optional passcode that you can enter manually into the Zoom app. This is particularly useful if you receive a text invitation on your phone but want to Zoom using another device, such as your tablet or computer.

(**1**) When it's time for the meeting, launch the Zoom app on your computer or mobile device or, from the Zoom website, click Join a Meeting. Sign in, if necessary, and then select the Home or (on some devices) Meet & Chat tab.

(**2**) Click or tap the Join icon.

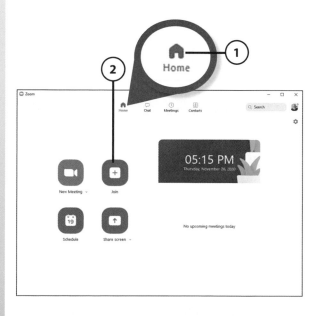

3 Enter the meeting ID into the Meeting ID field.

4 Accept or change your name.

5 Click or tap Join.

6 If prompted for a passcode or password, enter it and then click or tap OK or Join Meeting.

7 You may be placed in a virtual waiting room until admitted by the host. If so, wait for the host to admit you to the meeting.

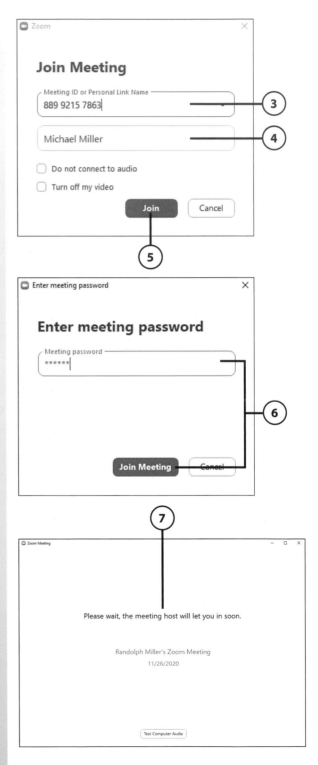

(**8**) Once you're admitted to the
meeting, you're ready to go.

Switch Cameras

If you're Zooming from a phone or tablet,
you can opt to use the front camera (the
one facing you) or the rear camera (to view
things on the other side of the room). Tap
the Switch Camera icon to switch from one
camera to another.

Switch Views

When you're in a Zoom meeting, you have the choice of viewing the other participants in one of two views:

- Active Speaker View (on some devices, called Speaker View) puts the person currently speaking in the large video window, with you in a thumbnail (on a mobile device) or up to three other participants in smaller thumbnails (on a computer). In this view, the person in the large window changes, depending on who's talking.

- Gallery View displays a large number of participants (on a computer, up to 49 at a time; fewer on devices with smaller screens) in a grid layout. The person currently speaking is highlighted with a green border. If there are more participants than can fit on screen, you scan scroll through additional participants by swiping with your finger on touchscreen devices or clicking the right or left arrows on a computer.

Active Speaker View on a computer

Active Speaker View on a tablet

Active Speaker View on a phone

Gallery View on a computer

Gallery View on a tablet

Gallery View on a phone

Change Gallery Order

When you're in Gallery View on a computer or tablet, you can change the order of the thumbnails displayed, which is great for putting the most active speakers up front. Just click or tap and drag any thumbnail to a new position in the grid. New participants are automatically added to the bottom right of the grid.

On a tablet, you can also display an expanded Active Speaker View. Just drag the + button in the top-left corner of your thumbnail picture to the left, and you will see four thumbnails across the bottom of the screen. Drag the + button back to the right to return to normal Active Speaker View, or tap or click the − button to remove your thumbnail completely.

Drag to expand or contract

Tap or click to remove thumbnail(s)

Expanded Active Speaker View on a tablet

Use the following techniques to switch the view on various devices:

(1) If you're on a computer, click the View button and select the view you want.

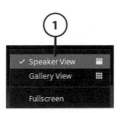

2 If you're on a tablet, tap Switch to Active Speaker View/Gallery View to switch between views.

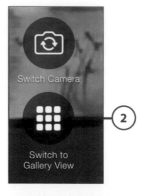

3 If you're on a phone, Active Speaker View displays by default. Swipe to the left to switch to Gallery View and continue swiping left to view additional participants.

4 Swipe to the right to view participants you've previously seen. Continue swiping to the right to return to Active Speaker View.

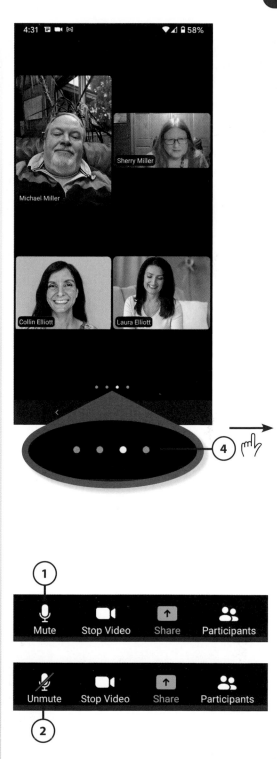

Mute Your Microphone

Sometimes in a meeting you don't want the other participants to hear what's happening in your (physical) room. It's common to mute your microphone when you're not talking. (When your microphone is muted, you can still hear what other participants are saying.)

1 Click or tap the Mute Audio icon to mute your microphone. (When you're muted, this icon has a slash through it.)

2 Click or tap the Unmute Audio icon to unmute your microphone so you can talk.

Turn Off Your Camera

Just as you can mute your microphone, you can also turn off your device's camera. This lets you do whatever you need to do without other meeting participants seeing you.

Audio and Video Are Separate

You can mute your audio and turn off video separately, so that people can still see you with your microphone muted or still hear you with your camera stopped. If you want to be totally invisible, you can mute your device's audio and turn off the video.

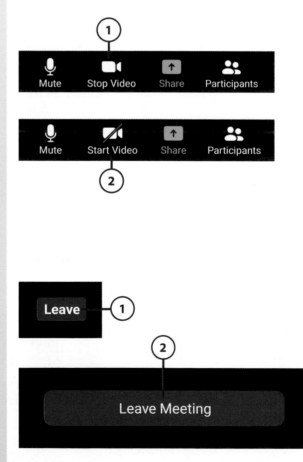

(1) Click or tap the Stop Video icon to turn off your device's camera. (When the camera is turned off, this icon has a slash through it.)

(2) Click or tap the Start Video icon to restart your device's camera.

Leave a Meeting

When a meeting officially ends, you'll be automatically disconnected from it, along with all other participants. You can, however, leave a meeting before it officially ends.

(1) Tap or mouse over the screen to display the chat controls; then click or tap the red Leave icon.

(2) Click or tap Leave Meeting.

>>>Go Further

RAISE YOUR HAND

In a large Zoom meeting, you may be one of dozens or hundreds of participants. If you want to get the attention of the hosts, you can't just speak up—especially if everybody's audio is muted. Instead, you can virtually raise your hand within Zoom.

When you're participating in a very large Zoom meeting where all the content is controlled by the hosts—often called a *webinar*—the option to indicate a raised hand changes a little from what you're typically used to. On a mobile device, you see options for Raise Hand, Chat, and Q&A; on a computer, you see a separate section for Webinar Controls, which includes the Raise Hand control.

To get the host's attention in a webinar, you need to click or tap the Raise Hand control. On a Windows PC, you can use the Ctrl+Y keyboard shortcut; on a Mac, Option+Y does the same thing.

Once you've virtually raised your hand, the webinar's host is notified that you'd like to say something. If the host allows you talk, remember to unmute your audio before speaking. (Note that not all hosts or webinars encourage audience participation.)

Hosting a Zoom Meeting

Anyone with a Zoom account can host a Zoom meeting. All you need is your device and the phone numbers or email addresses of the people you want to meet with.

Start an Instant Meeting

An instant meeting is one that you start immediately. It's not scheduled in advance.

Anyone can start an instant meeting. Once you've started one, you can invite participants.

(1) From the Home or Meet & Chat tab, click or tap New Meeting.

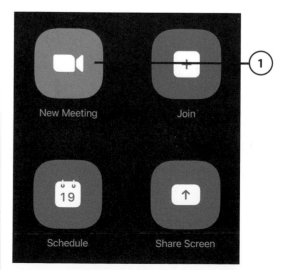

(2) If you're prompted to connect or use your device's audio and/or video, do so; then (if required) tap Start a Meeting.

(3) Your meeting is now live, with you as the only participant. (Read on to learn how to invite other people to your meeting.)

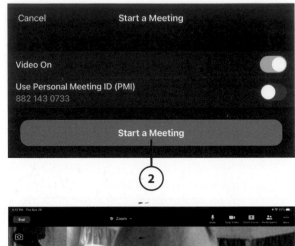

Invite Participants via Email

Once you've started a meeting, you need to invite other people to participate. You can invite one or more participants via email or text. This task covers email invitations.

(1) From within a meeting, click or tap Participants.

2 Click or tap Invite.

3 On your computer, click to select the Email tab; then select your email service. (In most cases, you should select Default Email.)

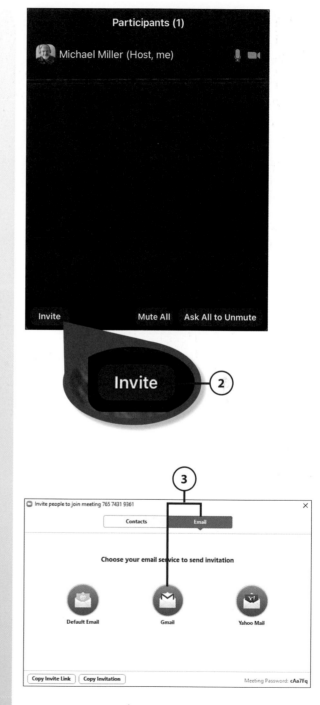

(4) On Android phones, tap your email service.

(5) On your tablet or iPhone, tap Send Email.

(6) You see a new email message with the meeting information already entered. Enter the email address(es) of your desired participant(s) and click or tap to send the invitation.

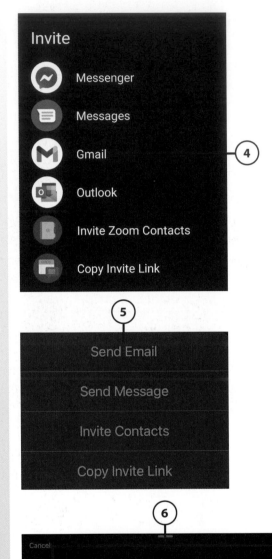

Invite

Messenger

Messages

Gmail

Outlook

Invite Zoom Contacts

Copy Invite Link

Send Email

Send Message

Invite Contacts

Copy Invite Link

Cancel

Please join Zoom meeting in progress

To:

Cc/Bcc, From: molehillgroup@icloud.com

Subject: Please join Zoom meeting in progress

Join Zoom Meeting
https://us04web.zoom.us/j/75667906486?
pwd=bDN0MG5wNFQ5N0tMeWVBS2hYNlh3Zz09

Meeting ID: 756 6790 6486
Passcode: Uru6S2

Invite Participants via Text

If you're Zooming from your phone or a tablet that has a messaging app, you can text an invitation to your desired participants. Follow these steps:

1. Tap Participants.
2. Tap Invite.
3. Tap your messaging app to open the messaging screen. (On an iPhone or iPad, tap Send Message.)
4. Select your recipient(s).

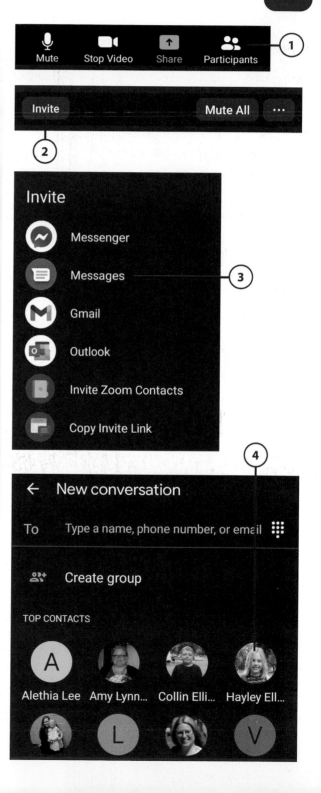

(5) The information about the meeting appears as a text message. Tap to send the text.

> **Click**
> **https://us04web.zoom.us**
> **/j/77387728763?pwd=**
> **ZXowN1pjSUgraXdmMkR**

Schedule a Meeting in Advance

It's also common to set up Zoom meetings in advance. You might want to Zoom with your grandkids on Thursday at 7:00 p.m., or maybe you have a regularly scheduled book club meeting over Zoom every Wednesday at 8:00 p.m. Zoom lets you schedule meetings so others can plan to attend.

(1) From the Home or Meet & Chat tab, click or tap Schedule. The Schedule Meeting window opens. (It looks different on different devices.)

(2) Enter a name or topic for the meeting.

(3) Enter the start date and time.

(4) Enter the duration or the end time of the meeting—up to 40 minutes, on a free account.

(5) If it's a recurring meeting (on the same day every week or month or the same time every day), click or tap Recurring Meeting or Repeat and select how often it repeats.

(6) Select whether you want Zoom to generate an automatic meeting ID or use your personal ID. (In most instances, let Zoom generate the ID automatically for better security.)

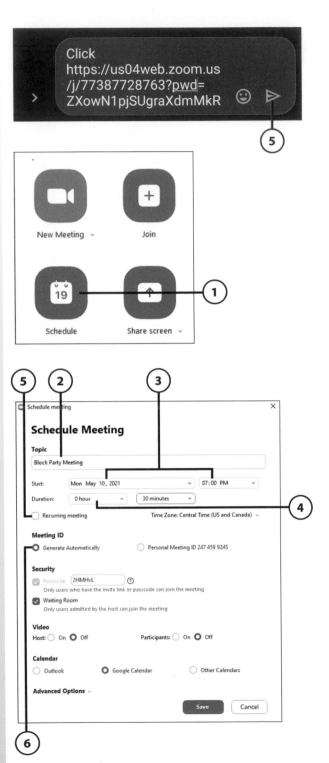

(7) Zoom recommends that you require a password or passcode to enter your meeting. You can accept Zoom's automatically generated passcode or manually enter your own passcode. This is recommended (and required for some accounts); otherwise, anyone with the meeting ID can enter the meeting.

(8) Make sure Waiting Room is checked or enabled. (Using the waiting room adds a layer of security to your meeting by letting you keep out uninvited participants.)

(9) Select whether you want the host video (your video) on or off. (You can change this during the course of a meeting, if you want.)

(10) Select whether you want participants' video on or off. (You can also change this during the course of a meeting.)

(11) Select if you want this meeting added to a specific calendar app.

(12) On a computer, click to open Advanced Options.

(7)

Schedule meeting   ✕

Schedule Meeting

Topic

Block Party Meeting

Start: Mon May 10, 2021   ⌄   07:00 PM   ⌄

Duration: 0 hour   ⌄   30 minutes   ⌄

☐ Recurring meeting   Time Zone: Central Time (US and Canada) ⌄

Meeting ID

◉ Generate Automatically   ◯ Personal Meeting ID 247 459 9245

Security

☑ Passcode   2HMHvL   ⑦
Only users who have the invite link or passcode can join the meeting

☑ Waiting Room
Only users admitted by the host can join the meeting   ⑨

Video

Host: ◯ On ◉ Off   Participants: ◯ On ◉ Off ————— ⑩

Calendar

◯ Outlook   ◉ Google Calendar   ◯ Other Calendars

Advanced Options ⌄

                                        Save   Cancel

⑧   ⑫   ⑪

(13) If you want participants to be able to join before you do, select Allow Participants to Join Anytime.

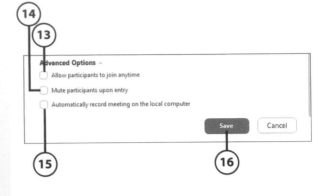

(14) If you want participants' sound to be automatically muted when they log on (best for larger meetings), select Mute Participants Upon Entry.

(15) On a computer, if you want to record the meeting, select Automatically Record Meeting on the Local Computer.

(16) Click Save.

Next Steps

What happens next depends on your device. You may see a New Event screen, be transferred to your device's calendar or scheduling app, or be prompted to invite others via email. Follow the onscreen instructions to invite others to your meeting.

>>>Go Further
ZOOMBOMBING

Zoom has had privacy issues with unwanted attendees popping into supposedly private meetings. This is called *Zoombombing*, and it can happen when a meeting isn't secured by a passcode and automatically generated meeting ID. If you use the same personal ID for every meeting you create and don't require passwords to log in, anyone who knows your personal meeting ID can easily enter any future meeting you create.

To avoid Zoombombing, do three things. First, always have Zoom automatically generate a unique ID for each new meeting. Second, require participants to enter a unique passcode. And, third, enable Zoom's waiting room function so that you can see who wants to join before they enter—and deny entry to anyone you didn't invite.

Manage a Meeting

Once your meeting has started, you need to keep things moving. Zoom offers several ways to manage a meeting in progress.

(1) When you launch a new meeting, if you've enabled the virtual waiting room option, participants who log in must wait until you admit them into the meeting. As each participant enters, click or tap Admit to admit each one into the meeting. You may see a notification for each new participant or, on a computer, use the Participants panel to admit them individually or as a group. (If you haven't enabled the waiting room option, participants are immediately admitted to the meeting.)

(2) To view a list of participants, click or tap Participants.

Participants

Participants in a Zoom meeting are listed in this order: host, you (if you're not the host), participants with no names, unmuted participants (alphabetically), and muted participants (alphabetically).

(3) To mute the audio of a specific participant, tap or mouse over that person's name and select Mute.

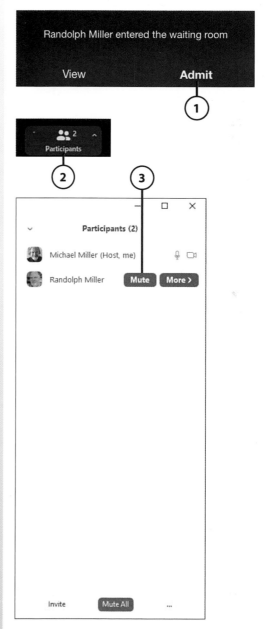

4 To mute the audio of all participants except yourself, tap or click Mute All. (If you're asked to confirm this, do so. You may also be asked to indicate if users can unmute themselves.)

5 To unmute some or all participants, tap or click the Mute or Mute All button again.

6 To view more meeting settings on a computer, click More (three dots) at the bottom of the Participants pane. On other devices, tap More in the main chat controls and then tap Meeting Settings.

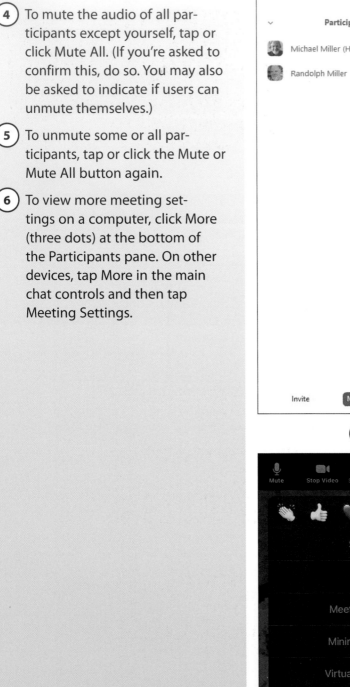

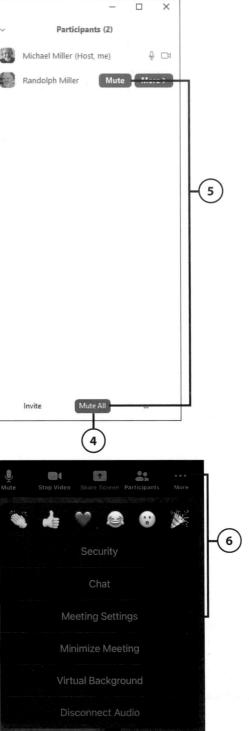

7 To play a sound when a new participant enters the meeting or an existing participant leaves the meeting, select Play Join and Leave Sound (or, on a computer, Play Sound When Someone Joins or Leaves).

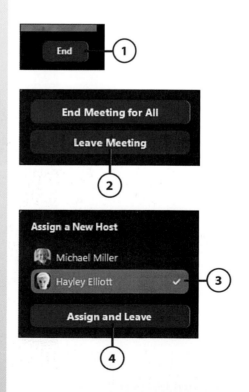

Assign Another Host and Leave the Meeting on a Computer

What do you do if you are the host and need to leave the meeting before it's over? Zoom lets you pass the host control to another participant so they can control the meeting while you leave.

1 From within the meeting, click the red End button.

2 Click Leave Meeting.

3 When prompted, select the person you want to assign as host.

4 Click Assign and Leave.

Assign Another Host and Leave the Meeting on a Phone or Tablet

Passing host control and leaving a meeting is a little different if you're Zooming on a phone or tablet.

(1) Tap Participants to display a list of all participants.

(2) Tap the name of the participant you want to assign as host.

(3) Tap Make Host.

(4) Tap Yes or OK to confirm your decision.

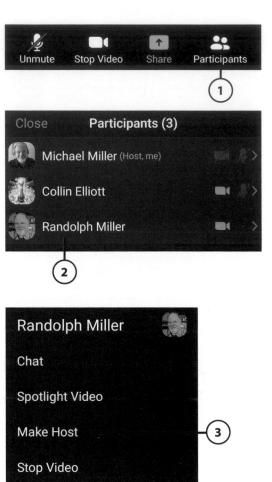

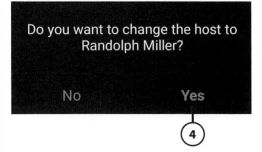

(5) Return to the meeting screen and tap the red Leave button.

(6) If prompted, tap Leave Meeting.

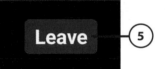

End a Meeting Early

Only a host can end a meeting. You can end a meeting before its designated end time or just allow 40 minutes to transpire, and the meeting will end automatically.

(1) From within the meeting, click or tap the red End button.

(2) Click or tap End Meeting for All.

Advanced Features

Zoom includes many advanced features you can use as either a participant or a host. Learn more in Chapter 4, "Getting More Out of Zoom."

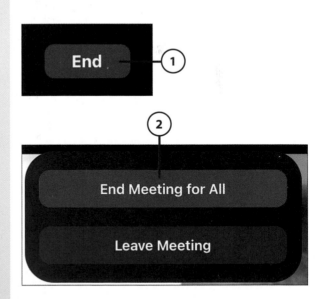

4

Getting More Out of Zoom

Chapter 3 covers enough about Zoom that you can participate in and even host Zoom meetings. This chapter covers all the advanced features of Zoom that can make Zoom meetings more fun and productive.

Advanced Features for Participants

When you're participating in a one-on-one or group Zoom meeting, it's easy enough to sit in your chair, listen to the other person or people, and speak up when you need to. There are a few other features, however, that can help you get even more out of your Zoom experience.

Apply a Virtual Background on a Computer

This is one of the most fun options Zoom offers, and the one I'm asked about the most. Instead of the other participants looking at the messy room or blank wall behind you, you can add a virtual background that makes it appear as if you're somewhere else. It's actually easy to do—and you can choose from Zoom's stock backgrounds or any image stored on your computer or mobile device. (You can even download other backgrounds from the Internet—see the "Where to Find Zoom Backgrounds" sidebar later in this chapter.)

Applying virtual backgrounds is slightly different when you're using Zoom on a computer versus using Zoom on a phone or tablet. This task covers using a computer.

Solid Color Background

Zoom's virtual backgrounds work best if you're sitting in front of a solid color background. They work even better if the background is green. (This is the "green screen effect" used in many movies and TV shows.) For best effect, you can set up an actual green screen by using a green cloth or paper backdrop, which you can find online or at a local photography store.

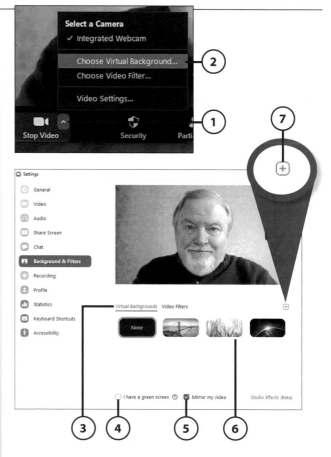

(1) During a Zoom meeting, click the up arrow next to the Stop Video button.

(2) Click Choose Virtual Background. This displays the Settings window.

(3) Select the Video Backgrounds tab.

(4) If you have a green screen background, check the I Have a Green Screen option.

(5) To view the virtual background as others see it, check Mirror My Video.

(6) Zoom's built-in backgrounds are displayed. You'll also see any other backgrounds you've recently selected. Click one of these backgrounds to use it. Or…

(7) To use another image as the virtual background, click the + and then click Add Image to display the Choose a Background Image dialog box.

Video Filters

Zoom also offers a selection of video filters that add fun images to your live picture in a Zoom meeting. Select the Video Filters tab to make a selection.

(8) Navigate to and select the image you want to use; then click Open.

(9) You see how the virtual background looks behind you.

(10) To return to your normal background, select None.

(11) Close the Settings window when you're done.

Background Videos

You can also use a video file as a virtual Zoom background—although it may be distracting to other participants. The video needs to be in MP4 or MOV format with a minimum resolution of 480 × 360 pixels and a maximum resolution of 1920 × 1080 pixels.

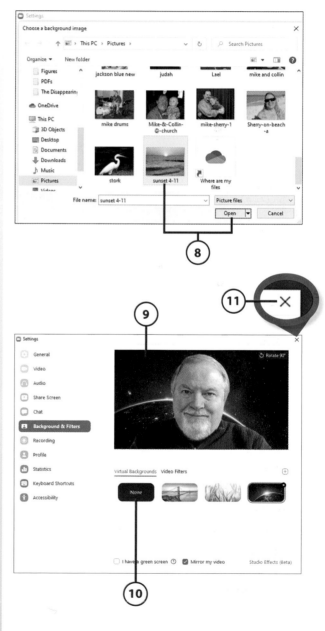

Apply a Virtual Background on a Phone or Tablet

As with many Zoom features, virtual backgrounds work slightly differently when you're Zooming with a phone or tablet.

1. During a Zoom meeting, tap the More button.

2. Tap Virtual Background.

3. Tap to select one of the available backgrounds. *Or...*

4. Tap the + to select another image stored on your device.

5. You see yourself with the virtual background applied. To return to your normal background, tap None.

6. Tap Close or the X in the top-right corner when you're done.

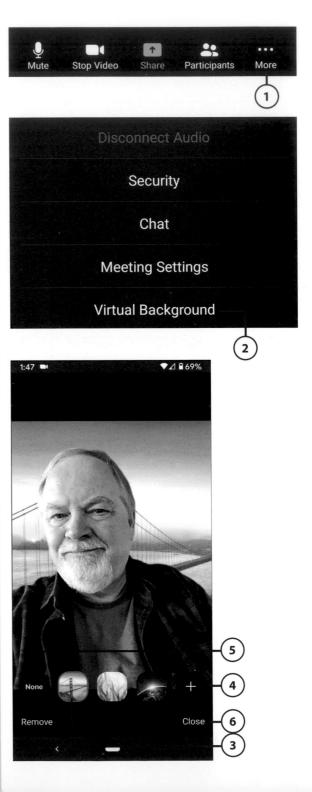

>>>*Go Further*
WHERE TO FIND ZOOM BACKGROUNDS

Zoom supplies a handful of built-in virtual backgrounds, and you can use any image stored on your computer or mobile device as a background. You also can download images from the Internet to use as your virtual background.

There are many websites that offer free images for your Zoom virtual backgrounds. Some of the most popular include

- Canva (www.canva.com/zoom-virtual-backgrounds/templates/)
- Getty Images (www.gettyimages.co.uk/resources/free-zoom-backgrounds)
- Hallmark Channel Virtual Backgrounds (www.hallmarkchannel.com/hallmark-channel-virtual-backgrounds)
- Modsy TV Show Interiors (blog.modsy.com/trends/pop-culture-designs/how-to-work-from-your-favorite-pop-culture-interiors/)
- Pixar Backgrounds (news.disney.com/pixar-video-backgrounds-available)
- Star Wars Backgrounds (www.starwars.com/news/star-wars-backgrounds)
- Unsplash (www.unsplash.com/s/photos/zoom-background)
- West Elm Video Conference Backgrounds (www.westelm.com/pages/features/zoom-virtual-backgrounds/)
- Zoom Virtual Backgrounds (www.zoom.us/virtual-backgrounds)

Simply download the image you want to use to your computer or mobile device, then follow the previous instructions for applying a virtual background. The image should be listed along with the other photos on your device.

As fun as some of these backgrounds look, you might want to pick a background that doesn't draw too much attention to itself—and away from you. That means choosing a background that isn't too far out or too busy. Especially in business meetings, simpler backgrounds—or those that resemble an office or boardroom—work best.

React to the Meeting

When you're Zooming with one or more other people, you can "react" to what someone says or does with a virtual clap or thumbs up. When you do so, a corresponding icon appears onscreen for a few seconds.

(1) On a computer, click Reactions and then choose from the reactions displayed.

(2) On a mobile device, tap More to see a selection of reactions.

(3) Tap the reaction you want to display.

Hide Self View

By default, your own live picture appears as a thumbnail on the Zoom screen. You may want to hide your live thumbnail, however, to avoid the temptation to look at yourself instead of others in the chat. To hide self view on a computer, mouse over your live thumbnail, click More (three dots), then select Hide Self View. On a tablet, tap the minus-sign (–) at the top-right corner of your live thumbnail. (Unfortunately, you can't hide self view on a phone.)

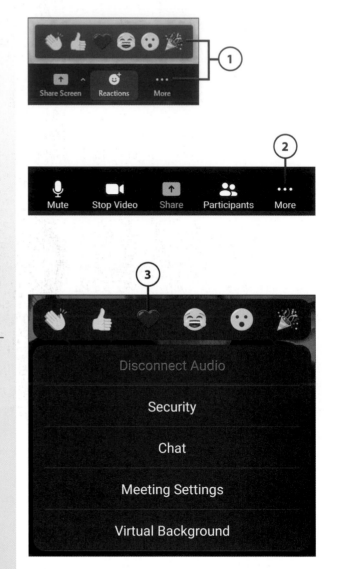

Chat with Other Participants on a Computer

When you're in a larger meeting, you might want to have a side conversation with one or more participants by using Zoom's Chat feature to send public messages to the whole group or private messages to one or more other users in a separate Chat window.

The chat function is slightly different on different devices. This task covers how to chat on a computer.

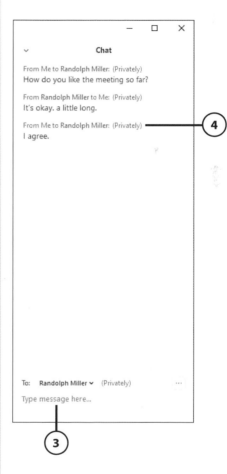

Private Messages

Private Zoom chat messages are viewable only by you and the person or people you're chatting with. Others, including the host, cannot see these messages. (The host can see any messages you send to all participants, however.)

1. Click Chat at the bottom of the screen. This displays a Chat window to the side of the screen.

2. Click the To field and select who you want to chat with. You can choose to chat with Everyone or specific participants.

3. Enter your message into the Type Message Here field and then press Enter.

4. The text message appears in the main Chat window.

5 When new chat messages are sent to you, the Chat button flashes orange and you see a preview of the message. Click this preview to open the Chat window and view the complete message. (If the Chat window is already open, you may not see this alert and preview.)

Chat with Other Participants on a Phone or Tablet

Chatting is a little different when you have a smaller screen, like on a smartphone or tablet. Here's how it works:

1 Tap More.

2 Tap Chat. You now see a separate Chat screen.

3 Tap the Send To field and select who you want to chat with. You can choose to chat with Everyone or specific participants.

4 Enter your message into the Tap Here to Chat field.

5 Tap Send to send the message.

6 The text message appears on the main Chat screen.

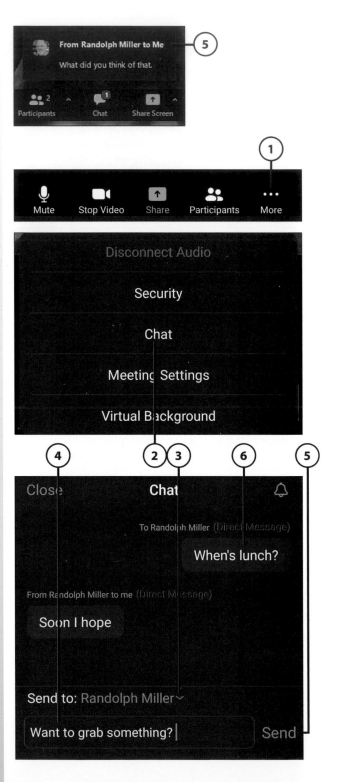

(7) When you receive a new chat message, a preview of that message appears at the bottom of the Zoom meeting screen. Tap to view the entire message.

Share Screen Content on a Computer

During a video chat, you may want to share the content of your screen with other meeting participants. For example, you may want to give a PowerPoint presentation, show pictures or a video, read a story together, or review a document. You can do this easily, although it's a tad different between the computer and mobile versions of Zoom.

Who Can Share?

By default the host can share his or her screen content. If the host enables it, other participants can also share their screens, although not all hosts want everyone sharing their screens.

This task explains how to share screen content on a computer. You can share either the entire screen or the contents of any open window. If you're doing the latter, make sure you have the app or file you want to share open on your desktop.

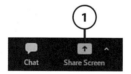

(1) From within the Zoom meeting, click Share Screen to open the Select a Window or Application window.

(**2**) Select the Basic tab.

(**3**) Click the window you want to share. (You can also opt to share the entire desktop or open a virtual whiteboard for drawing.)

(**4**) Click Share.

Whiteboard

In Zoom, a whiteboard is essentially an onscreen page where the host and participants (if allowed) can write, draw, or otherwise add notes and annotations during the course of a meeting. All participants can see the contents of the whiteboard as part of Zoom's screensharing feature.

Share the Sound

If you're sharing a video or presentation that has sound, you can share that audio (along with the meeting's regular audio) by checking the Share Computer Sound option.

(**5**) Your Zoom window is now changed to a thumbnail, and the window you're sharing is front and center on your desktop. You see a green You Are Screen Sharing bar at the top of the screen. All meeting participants see the window you're sharing.

(**6**) When you're done sharing, click the red Stop Share button.

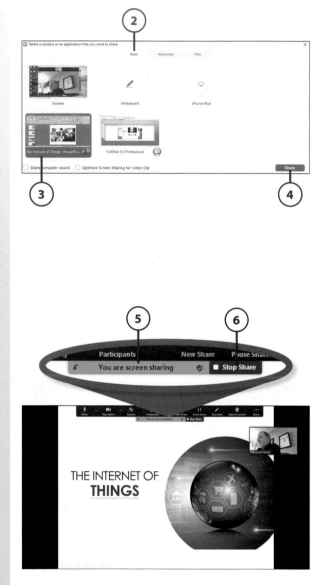

Share Screen Content on a Phone or Tablet

Sharing content on a phone or tablet is similar to sharing on a computer. You can share the contents of a web page, your device's screen, your device's camera, a document stored on your device, content stored on a cloud storage service (such as Google Drive, iCloud, and Microsoft OneDrive), or a virtual whiteboard for drawing.

① From within the meeting, tap Share or Share Screen.

② Tap the type of item you want to share.

③ Tap the specific item you want to share.

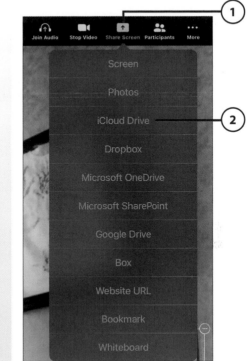

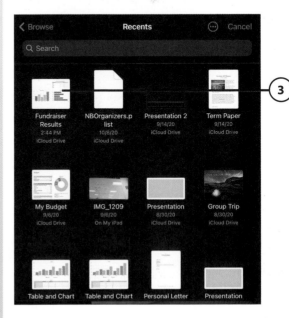

(4) Your screen now displays the
item you're sharing. All meeting
participants see the same screen.

(5) When you're done sharing, tap
the screen to display Zoom's chat
controls and then tap Stop Share.

Advanced Features for Hosts

If you're hosting a Zoom meeting, you can take advantage of several advanced
features that give you more control over your meetings.

Enable or Disable Options for Participants

As a meeting host, you can enable or
disable a variety of settings for meeting participants. For example, you can
allow participants to enter the meeting
without your permission, share their
screens, unmute themselves, and chat
with others—or not.

(1) From within a meeting on a
phone or tablet, tap More, then
tap Security.

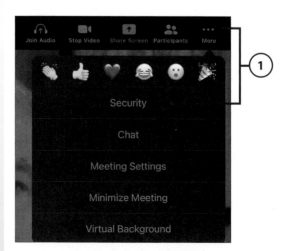

(**2**) From within a meeting on a computer, click Security to display the pop-up menu.

(**3**) Enable Lock Meeting to disallow any new participants from entering.

(**4**) Deselect Enable Waiting Room to allow new participants to join the meeting directly without your host approval.

(**5**) Select Hide Profile Pictures to hide participants' profile pictures and instead display a generic graphic. (This is a good idea if you think users might have distracting or inappropriate profile pictures.)

(**6**) Enable Share Screen to allow participants to share their screen content.

(**7**) By default, participants can chat with all other participants. To disable the chat function from a computer, deselect Chat. To limit the chat function on a phone or tablet, tap Chat With and select No One, Host Only, Everyone Publicly, or Everyone (default).

(**8**) Deselect Rename Themselves if you don't want participants to rename themselves—that is, change the name that accompanies their live pictures.

(**9**) Deselect Unmute Themselves if you want participants to remain muted unless you unmute them.

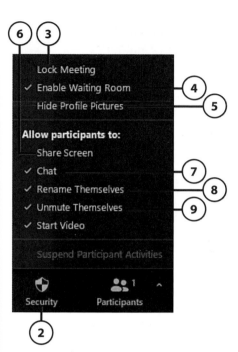

10 Deselect Start Video if you don't want to see live video of participants.

11 Click or tap Suspend Participant Activities to turn off everyone's audio and video, stop all screen sharing, and lock the meeting. (This is a good way to regain control of a meeting that may have gone off the rails.)

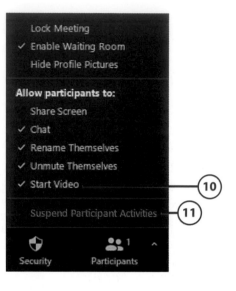

Transfer Host Duties

You don't have to stay the host for the entire meeting. Zoom lets you transfer host duties at any time to another participant.

1 Click or tap Participants.

2 Tap the name of the person you want to be the new host. (Or, on a computer, mouse over that person's name and select the More—three-dot—icon.)

3 Click or tap Make Host and confirm the action when prompted.

Record a Zoom Meeting on Your Computer

If you're hosting a Zoom meeting on your computer, you can opt to record your meetings, which is good if you have people who are unable to attend in real time but can watch the proceedings later. All recordings are stored on your computer's hard drive, so you can share them from there.

Paid Accounts

If you have a free Zoom account, you can record meetings only from your computer, not from a mobile device. If you or your business has a paid Zoom account, however, you can record from either a computer or mobile device, and you have the option of saving your recordings locally or to the cloud.

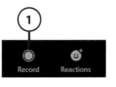

1. From within the meeting, tap Record.

2. Recording starts, and recording controls appear at the top of the Zoom window. Everything on your screen and everything people say will be recorded.

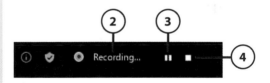

3. To pause the recording, click the Pause button. Click this button again to resume recording.

4. Click Stop to stop recording at any point in your meeting. (The recording also stops automatically when your meeting ends.) The recording is converted to MP4 format and stored in the documents/zoom/ folder.

Sharing a Zoom Recording

To share a locally stored Zoom recording, you need to upload the file to a cloud storage service, such as Google Drive, iCloud, or Microsoft OneDrive. You can then share a link to the video file with those who want to view it.

Managing Zoom Contacts

When you launch or schedule a new Zoom meeting, you can add participants' email addresses manually each time, or you can make things easier by adding frequent participants to your Zoom contacts list. It's easier to send meeting invitations to your contacts than it is to enter their information by hand.

Add a Zoom Contact

When you add a person to your Zoom contacts, that person receives an invitation, either via email (if they don't currently have a Zoom account) or within the Zoom app (if they do have an account). When that person accepts the invitation, they're added to your contacts list.

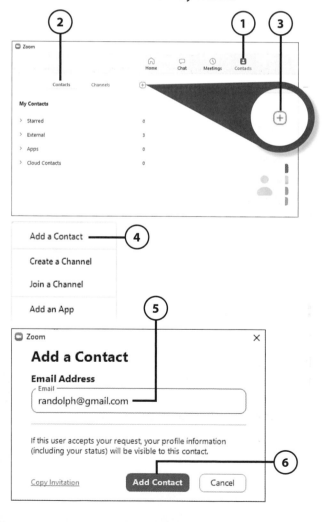

1. From the main Zoom screen, select the Contacts tab.

2. In the left panel (or, on a phone, the next screen), select Contacts.

3. Click or tap the + icon.

4. Select Add a Contact.

5. Enter the contact's email address.

6. Click or tap Add or Add Contact.

Meet One-on-One with a Contact

Once someone is added to your Zoom contacts list, it's easy to launch a one-on-one meeting with that person.

1. From the main Zoom screen, select the Contacts tab.

2. In the left panel (or, on a phone, the next screen), select Contacts.

3. Click or tap the contact with whom you want to meet.

4. Click or tap Meet. Zoom launches a new meeting and invites that person.

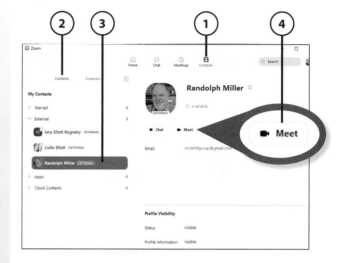

Invited to the Waiting Room

People you invite to a Zoom meeting still have to enter through the waiting room if you've enabled that safety precaution. They are not automatically admitted into the meeting.

Invite a Contact to a Group Meeting

It's easy to invite people on your contacts list to a group Zoom meeting.

1. From within a meeting, click or tap Participants.

2. Click or tap Invite.

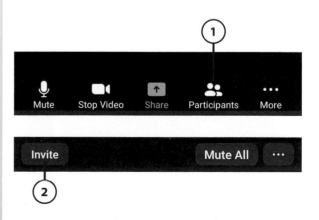

(3) Click or tap Invite Contacts or Invite Zoom Contacts.

(4) Select those contacts you want to invite.

(5) Click or tap Invite. Your selected contacts will receive invitations to the meeting.

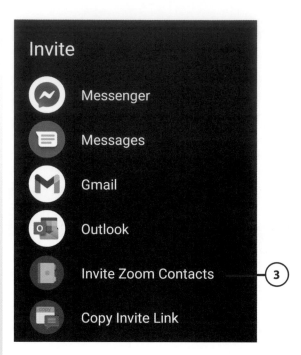

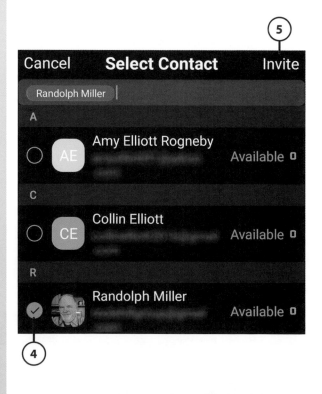

>>>*Go Further*

BREAKOUT ROOMS

If you're using the paid version of Zoom or attending a meeting hosted by someone with the paid version, you may encounter a feature called breakout rooms. A breakout room is a smaller subset of a larger meeting where select participants leave the main meeting to conduct smaller breakout sessions. It's a way to break larger meetings into more manageable rooms.

Many hosts use breakout rooms to conduct smaller, more focused meetings or just encourage conversations between a smaller group of participants. It's the virtual equivalent of attending a big real-world conference and then breaking out into smaller sessions in separate rooms.

In this chapter, you learn how to video chat on iPhones, iPads, and Macs with Apple's FaceTime.

→ Understanding Apple FaceTime
→ Video Chatting with FaceTime
→ Using Group FaceTime for Larger Meetings

5

Using FaceTime

FaceTime is a video chat platform exclusively for Apple devices. It's as easy to use as making a call on your iPhone or even iPad. You can also use FaceTime to video chat on your Mac computer.

Understanding Apple FaceTime

First things first. FaceTime is available only on Apple devices—iPads, iPhones, and Mac computers. To chat with people who don't have an Apple device, you have to use another video chat platform, such as Facebook Messenger, Google Duo, Skype, or Zoom.

Apple introduced FaceTime back in 2010 for iPhones, although over the years the platform expanded to include other Apple devices—the iPod touch first, then iPads and Mac computers.

Because of its iPhone origins, FaceTime was initially for one-on-one chats only. The ability to chat with more than one user was added in 2018. What Apple calls Group FaceTime allows up to 32 participants.

Even though FaceTime was launched and promoted as a video chat platform, it also enables audio calls between users of Apple devices. As such, it can function as a substitute to normal cellular calls. In a situation where you have a good Wi-Fi connection but poor cellular service, a FaceTime audio-only call would be a good choice.

Video Chatting with FaceTime

FaceTime is, like many Apple designs, easy and intuitive to use. Initiating or answering a video chat with FaceTime is every bit as easy as making or answering a phone call. It's a great video chat platform for those people who aren't tech savvy—as long as all parties are using Apple devices.

Answer a FaceTime Request

If you have an iPhone, iPad, or Mac, you should have the FaceTime app installed on your device by default, allowing anyone else with an Apple device to call you via FaceTime. You answer a FaceTime call by pressing an icon and talking, just as you would answer a phone call.

(1) When someone calls you via FaceTime, you see a FaceTime panel at the top of the screen. Tap Accept to accept the call. *Or...*

(2) Tap Decline to reject the call.

Ralph Miller
FaceTime Video

Start a Video Chat

It's also easy to initiate a video chat with another person.

(1) When you launch the FaceTime app on an iPad, you see yourself via your device's front-facing camera. Overlaid on the left side of the screen is a list of people with whom you've recently chatted. To chat again with one of the people listed, tap that person's name.

(2) When you launch the FaceTime app on an iPhone, you see a list of those people with whom you've recently chatted. To chat with one of these people, tap the person's name, number, or email address. *Or…*

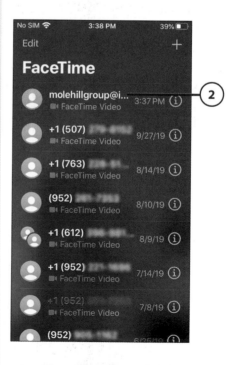

3 To chat with someone new, tap the + icon on the initial screen.

4 Start typing a person's name, phone number, or email address into the To box.

5 As you type, matching contacts are displayed. Select the person you want from this list, or finish typing the person's name, email address, or phone number.

6 Tap the Video button, and FaceTime dials the other person. (If you'd rather make a voice call, tap the Audio button.)

7 If that person is available and answers, you see that person onscreen. A small thumbnail in the corner of the screen displays what the other person is seeing (you). Have a nice conversation!

8 Tap Mute to mute the microphone. Tap the button again to unmute yourself.

9 Tap Flip on an iPhone or iPad to switch from the front to the rear camera. Tap this button again to switch back.

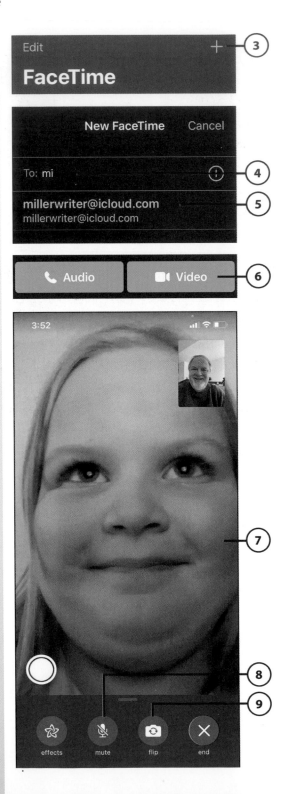

(10) Tap the Effects button to apply fun filters and effects to your picture in a chat.

(11) Pull up the top of the chat controls and tap Camera Off to turn off the camera. Tap this button again to turn the camera back on.

(12) Tap the red End icon to end the chat.

>>>Go Further

USE MEMOJI

If you have an iPhone X or later or an iPad with Face ID, you can create a Memoji to match your personality and mood and then use that Memoji during a FaceTime video chat. A Memoji is an animated avatar that displays instead of your face onscreen but tracks all your facial movements. It makes it look like you have a funny animal head, or a robot head, or something similar.

Video chatting with a Memoji

To use Memoji in a FaceTime chat, tap the Effects button and then tap the Memoji you want to use. To stop using the Memoji, tap the X.

Using Group FaceTime for Larger Meetings

Group FaceTime lets you chat with up to 32 people at once. When you're invited to join a group chat, you see a notification in your device's Notification Center. Reply to the notification the same as you would with a normal FaceTime call.

Start a Group FaceTime Chat

Starting a Group FaceTime video chat is similar to launching a one-on-one FaceTime call. You just invite more people!

(1) From the initial FaceTime screen, tap the + icon in the top-right corner.

(2) Enter the names of the people you want to invite to the chat.

(3) Tap the Video button. FaceTime now dials the people you listed and begins the group video chat.

(4) All the people in the chat appear onscreen. To mute your microphone, tap Mute. Tap the button again to unmute your mic.

(5) Tap the red End icon to end the chat.

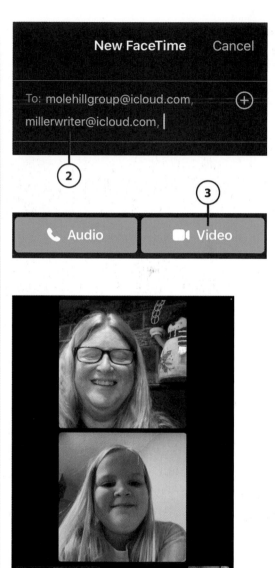

Add a Person to a Group Chat

FaceTime lets you add other people to an in-progress group chat.

1. From within a group chat, drag the top of the control panel up to expand it.

2. Tap Add Person.

3. Enter the name or email address of the person you want to add.

4. Tap Add Person to FaceTime.

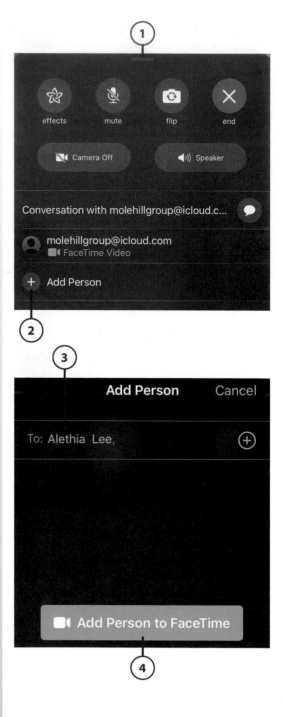

⑤ FaceTime dials the other people one by one and, when they answer, adds them to the chat.

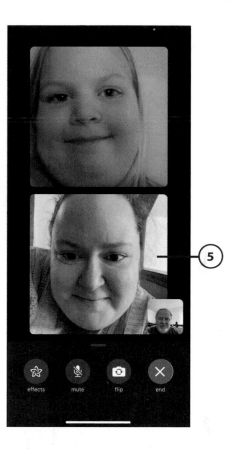

It's Not All Good

Troubleshooting FaceTime

If you try to make a FaceTime call, either from the FaceTime app or from within Apple's Messages app, and the FaceTime icon is grayed out, here are some things to try.

It's possible that your phone is not connected to either a Wi-Fi or cellular network. Open the iPhone's Settings app, tap Wi-Fi, and make sure Wi-Fi is enabled and connected and logged on to a working wireless network. Likewise, from the Settings app, tap Cellular and make sure Cellular Data is turned on.

It's also possible that FaceTime has not been disabled on your phone. Open the Settings app, scroll down and tap FaceTime, and then make sure the FaceTime option is "on" (green).

6

Using Facebook Messenger

If you're a Facebook user (and, since Facebook has more than 2.7 billion users worldwide, you may well be), you can video chat with other Facebook users via Facebook Messenger. Messenger is Facebook's messaging service, typically used for one-on-one and group texts, but it also has video chat functionality. Like other video chat platforms covered in this book, it is free. The only requirement is that you and the people you want to chat with are on Facebook.

Facebook Messenger is also available to users of Instagram, which Facebook owns. Plus, if you want to do larger group video chats, Facebook offers Messenger Rooms, which lets you chat with up to 50 people at one time.

Understanding Facebook Messenger

Facebook Messenger is Facebook's video chat service. If you're using Facebook on your computer, Facebook Messenger is integrated into the Facebook website. If you're using Facebook on your Android or Apple iOS phone or tablet, Messenger is a separate app from the regular Facebook app. Messenger lets you video chat with anyone on your Facebook friends list—or with any of your phone contacts who are also on Facebook.

On a phone, the Messenger app taps into your phone's contacts list and identifies those contacts who are also on Facebook. This means that you can video chat with any of your contacts who are also Facebook or Instagram users, even if they're not currently on your friends list. You can also use Messenger to video chat with people who have the Facebook Portal or Facebook Portal TV devices.

Facebook Portal

Learn more about Facebook Portal devices in Chapter 11, "Video Chatting with Facebook Portal, Amazon Echo Show, and Google Nest Hub Max."

Video Chatting with Facebook Messenger

While many Facebook users initially use Facebook Messenger for text messaging, its video chat functionality is becoming increasingly popular. This is due to the large number of people who are on Facebook every day and Messenger's ease of use. It also helps that Messenger's video chat functionality is quite easy to use; it's pretty much a one-button process to open a chat.

Facebook or Instagram Users Only

You have to be a Facebook or Instagram user to video chat with Facebook Messenger. If you don't use Facebook or Instagram, you can't chat with Messenger.

Start a Video Chat from the Messenger App on Your Phone or Tablet

If you're connecting to Facebook from your mobile phone or tablet, you use the Messenger app to video chat. You can chat with people who are connected to Facebook on their phones, tablets, or computers (assuming they have cameras connected to their computers, of course).

1. From within the Messenger app, tap the People tab to display the People page.

2. Tap the Active tab to view the All People icon to display a list of all of your Facebook friends who are currently online and available to chat. Tap the friend with whom you want to chat. A chat page for this person opens.

3. If this person has a phone or tablet or a computer with a camera, you see a camera icon; if the person is online and ready to chat, you'll see a green dot next to the camera icon. Tap this icon to start a video chat.

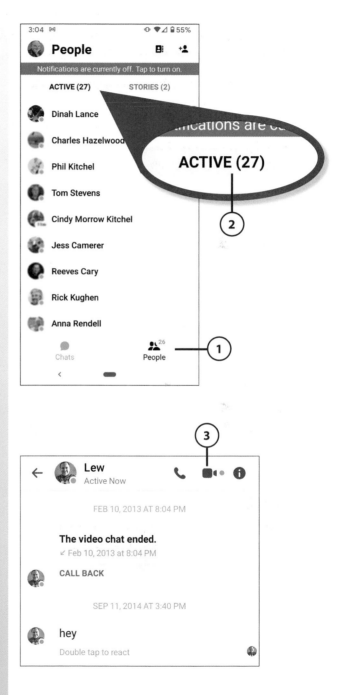

4 When your friend answers the call, you see that person's picture on your device's screen and the video chat begins. A small picture of you appears in the corner.

5 Tap the screen to display the chat controls.

6 Tap the switch button to switch between your device's front and rear cameras.

7 Tap the microphone button to mute your microphone; tap the button again to unmute your mic.

8 Tap the camera button to turn off your camera; tap the button again to turn your camera back on.

9 Tap the red End Call button to end the video chat.

Start a Video Chat from the Facebook Website

You can also engage in video chats from your desktop or laptop computer. For this to work, you need to be using Facebook in the Google Chrome, Microsoft Edge, or Opera web browsers. (It doesn't work in other browsers, including Apple's Safari browser.)

1 Scroll through your Contacts list at the bottom right of the Facebook home page and click the person with whom you want to chat. (Users who are currently online have a green dot next to their names.) A chat panel for this person opens.

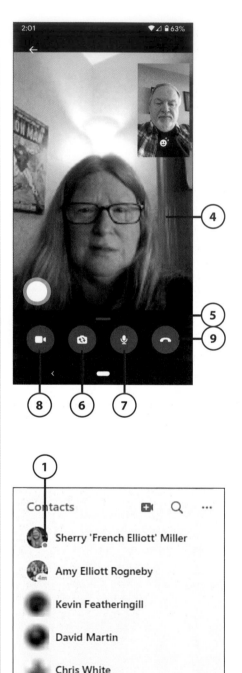

2 If your friend has a device with a camera, you'll see a camera icon at the top of the Chat panel. If this person is also online, you'll see a green dot next to the camera icon. Click this icon to initiate the video chat.

3 When your friend answers the call, Facebook displays the video chat window. Your friend appears in the main part of the window; your picture is in a smaller window in the corner of the screen.

4 Mouse over the screen to display the chat controls.

5 Click the mute button to mute your microphone; click the button again to unmute your mic.

6 Click the camera button to turn off your camera; click the button again to turn your camera back on.

7 When you're ready to close the chat, click the red End Call button.

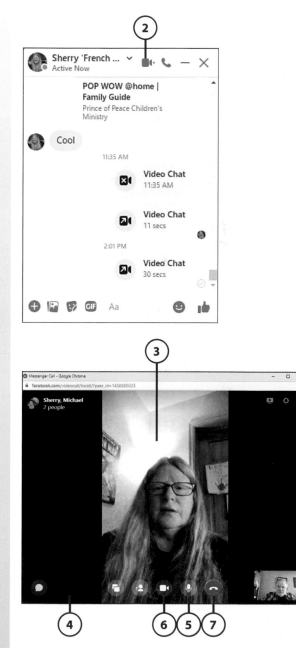

Answer a Video Call

Whether you're using the app or web version of Messenger, answering a video call is similar.

1. On a mobile device, you should see an onscreen notification. Tap Answer or Accept to join the call.

2. On a computer, you see an onscreen notification. Click Accept to join the chat.

3. On any device, click or tap Decline if you don't want to take the call.

Add Another Person to a Group Call

Facebook Messenger lets you add up to 50 Facebook users to an ongoing video chat to make it a group call.

1. On a mobile device, pull up the chat panel from the bottom of the screen and tap Add People.

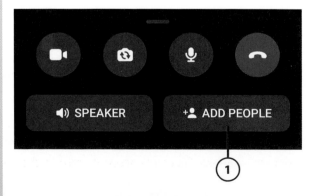

2) On a computer, click to display the chat controls and then click Add Group Members.

3) From the Add People screen, click or tap the person or persons you want to add to the group chat.

4) The person or persons you selected are added to the call. Click or tap End Call to exit the call.

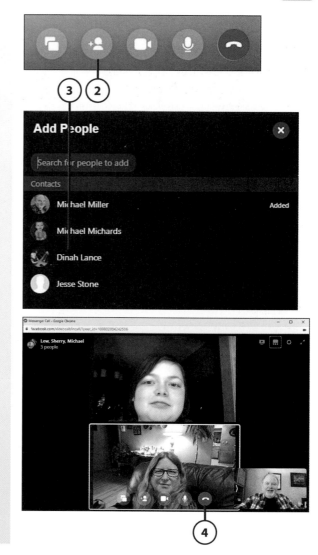

>>>Go Further
UNDERSTANDING THE DIFFERENCES

It's easy to get confused about Facebook Messenger and Messenger Rooms. Let's try to sort it all out.

Facebook Messenger is essentially a one-on-one chat platform, even though you can use it for small group chats. You and the people you chat with all need to be Facebook members; people who do not have Facebook accounts cannot chat with Messenger.

Messenger Rooms is designed as a chat platform for larger meetings (up to 50 people). Unlike regular Messenger, you don't have to be a Facebook member to participate in a Messenger Room (although you do have to be a Facebook member to host a Messenger Room).

Both Messenger and Messenger Rooms can be used from either the Messenger mobile app (on phones and tablets) or the Facebook website (on computers). Both platforms are free.

Group Chatting with Messenger Rooms

For even larger group meetings, use what Facebook calls Messenger Rooms. Unlike with normal Facebook Messenger, participants in Messenger Rooms do not need to be Facebook members.

In Messenger Rooms, you can have up to 50 participants with no time limits. The Room host must be a Facebook member, but the other participants don't have to be. You invite others to join with an email link, just like with Zoom, so that non-Facebook users can participate. Messenger Rooms also has some fun and useful features, including camera filters, mood lighting, and 360-degree backgrounds. In many instances, you will also be able to share your screen, as you can do in Zoom and Microsoft Teams.

Create a Messenger Room on a Computer

First, you need to create a Messenger Room for group video chats.

(1) Open the Facebook home page, go to your Contacts list, and click the New Room (camera) icon.

(2) You are now taken directly to your new Room. Any of your friends can join, or you can choose to invite specific people.

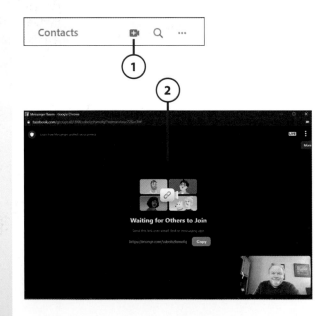

Create a Messenger Room on a Phone or Tablet

The process of creating a Messenger Room is slightly different on mobile devices.

(1) Tap to select the Chats tab.

(2) Tap Create Room. You see a screen with your Facebook friends displayed.

(3) Tap Invite for those friends you want to join your Room.

(4) Tap Join Room to enter your Room.

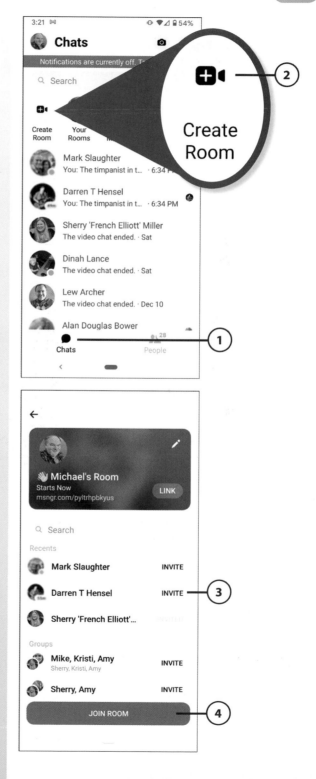

Invite Other Participants

With your Messenger Room open, you can invite others—including non-Facebook members—to the Room by sharing the link with them.

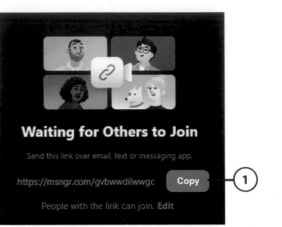

(1) On a computer, click the Copy button to copy the link to the Room. Then paste this link into an email message or Facebook Messenger text message to invite anyone to the Room.

(2) For most devices, in the Facebook Messenger mobile app, tap Share Link to see your Facebook friends list. For iPhones, you're prompted to select how you want to invite your friends—email, text, AirDrop, Messenger, and the like.

(3) Tap Invite next to the names of the people you want to invite.

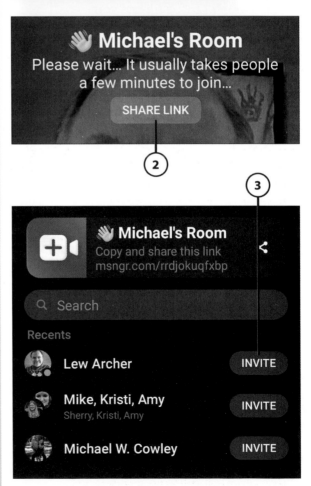

(**4**) When a person accepts your invitation, they're added to your Room.

④

Video Chat in a Messenger Room

(**1**) On a computer, click More and then toggle between Grid View (all speakers visible) and Speaker View (view current speaker large). (This option is not available in the Messenger mobile app.)

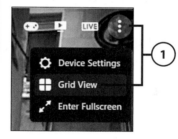

(**2**) Mouse over the screen on a computer or, in the Facebook mobile app, either tap or pull up from the bottom of the screen to display the chat controls. From here, you can mute and unmute the audio, turn the camera on and off, and—on a mobile device—switch between front and rear cameras.

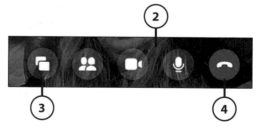

(**3**) On a computer, click the Share Your Screen icon to share the contents of your screen. You can opt to share your entire screen, a specific window, or a tab in your web browser. (This option may not be available on all systems.)

(**4**) To leave the Room, tap the red Leave Room button.

>>>*Go Further*

EFFECTS AND BACKGROUNDS

When you're using Messenger Rooms in the Messenger mobile app, you can add effects and backgrounds to your picture. Tap your thumbnail to see new options at the bottom of the screen.

Take a screenshot ——

Apply a photo filter

Apply silly facial — EFFECTS   BACKGROUNDS — Apply a virtual
effects   background

Messenger Room effects

Tap Effects to choose silly effects for your head. Tap Filter to apply a photo filter to your pictures. (On an iPhone, this is on the Lighting tab.) Tap Backgrounds to add a virtual background. Or tap the big white button to take a screenshot of the meeting in progress.

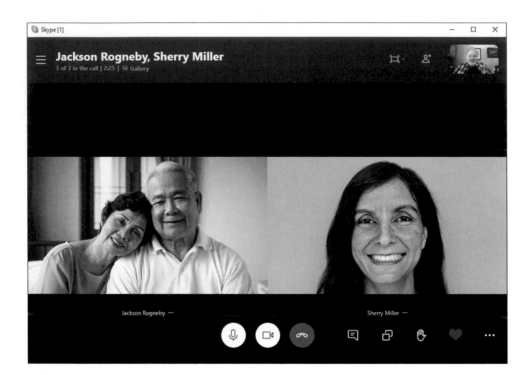

In this chapter, you learn how to use Microsoft's Skype platform for video chatting.

→ Understanding Skype
→ Video Chatting with Skype
→ Using Skype for Group Video Chats

Using Skype

Skype is a video chat service that connects to any device and across any platform—Apple and Android phones and tablets as well as Windows, Mac, and Chromebook computers. You can use Skype to conduct one-on-one chats as well as group calls for up to 50 participants, all with no time limits. Like other services covered in this book, Skype is free, although you need to have a Skype account, which is also free.

Understanding Skype

Skype was one of the first video chat services, launched in 2003. Originally an independent company, Skype is now owned and operated by Microsoft.

Skype has a history as a robust cross-platform communications service. Skype offers apps for Windows and Mac computers, Android and iOS phones and tablets, and even Microsoft's Xbox gaming console. You can also use Skype from any web browser. Today, Skype is used by more than 100 million people every month.

To use Skype, you need to either sign in with a Microsoft account or email address from Outlook or Hotmail (since they're all owned by Microsoft). You also can register for a Skype account, which is free. When you register, you get a unique Skype ID and username, which is how other Skype users see you. Even though you can use Skype from your browser, you'll probably want to install and use the free Skype app for your device.

Skype on the Web

You can use Skype from any web browser without signing into a Skype or Microsoft account. This chapter focuses on using the Skype desktop and mobile apps, but the browser-based version offers a similar experience.

Video Chatting with Skype

Once you're signed into Skype using its app, you can receive and launch video chats with any other Skype users, no matter what type of device they're using. You just need to have the Skype app open.

Accept a Video Call

When one of your contacts calls you for a video chat, you receive an onscreen notification.

Email Invitations

Someone who is not on your Skype contact list can also invite you to a Skype video chat via email. If you receive an email invitation, click the link in the message to join the chat, either via Skype's website or the Skype app.

1. You will receive an onscreen notification on your device that you have an incoming Skype call. To answer as a video call, tap or click the green Video icon. (On some mobile devices, just tap Accept.)

2. To answer as a voice call, with no video, click or tap the Phone icon.

3. You see the person calling you in the main part of the Skype window or screen. Your thumbnail is in the corner of the screen.

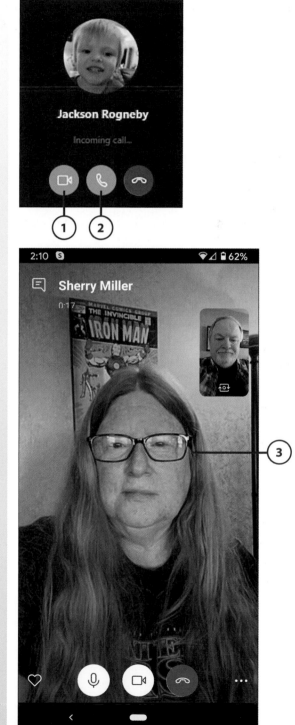

Add a Contact

Before you call someone with Skype, you have to add that person to your Skype contacts list. If you're using Skype on a phone, you can easily add your existing contacts to Skype by giving Skype permission to access your contacts.

You can also search for others who are Skype users. When you do this, you send them an invitation to be your Skype contact, which they have to accept before you can Skype them.

1. From within the Skype app, tap or click the Contacts tab. (On a computer, click the Contacts tab in the left panel.) Any contacts you've already added are displayed here.

2. In the Skype mobile app, select My Contacts to view your Skype contacts or All to view all the contacts on your phone.

3. Click or tap the Search icon and then enter a person's name to search for that person on Skype. (On an iPhone, just enter the person's name into the top-of-screen search bar.)

4. Skype displays people who match your query in both your contacts list and publicly on Skype. Click or tap the name of the person you want to contact.

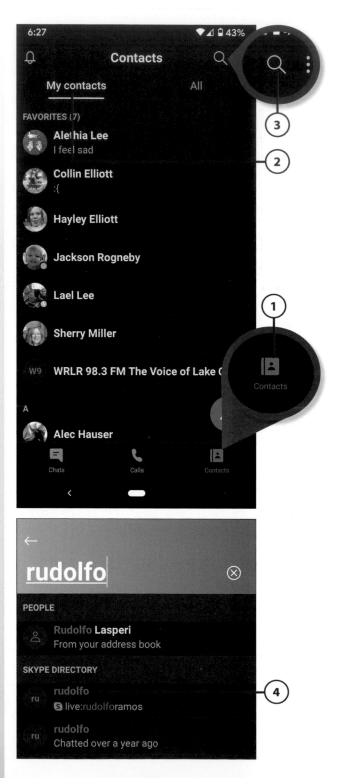

(5) To simply say "hi" to this contact, click or tap Say Hi.

(6) Otherwise, type a message to this person.

(7) Click Send. The person you selected now receives a request to become your Skype contact. If the person accepts your request, you'll be added to each other's contact lists. (People who decline are not added as contacts, so you can't Skype them.)

Accepting Contact Requests

Just as you can ask someone to be your Skype contact, other people can send contact requests to you. You have the option of accepting or declining any such request. Make sure it's someone you know before you accept.

Start a Video Chat

Starting a video chat is as easy as finding a contact and tapping a button.

(1) Select the Calls tab to display recent audio and video calls (on a computer, in the left panel).

(2) Click or tap the camera next to a person's name to call them again.

(3) Click or tap the New Call (telephone) button to chat with someone you haven't previously called.

(4) Select the person you want to chat with. To open a group video chat, select more than one person. *Or…*

(5) Enter that person's name into the Search box and then select the person from the search results.

(6) Click or tap the Call button.

(7) For a one-on-one chat, select Video Call. Skype calls the person you select. If you select multiple contacts to chat with, Skype goes immediately into the call.

Voice Calls

You can use Skype to make voice calls as well as video chats. To initiate a voice call instead of a video call, select Call instead of Video Call after clicking/tapping the Call button. Skype lets you call non-Skype users, but it charges 2.3 cents per minute for U.S. voice calls and sells subscriptions, starting at $2.99 per month, for unlimited voice calling. (Prices vary by the country you're calling.)

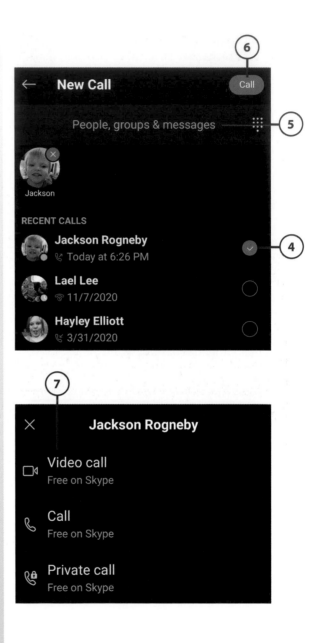

(8) When that person answers the call, you see a live picture of the person in the main part of the screen. (Your live picture appears smaller, in the corner of the screen.)

(9) Tap the screen (on a touchscreen device) or mouse over the screen (on a computer) to display the chat controls.

(10) Click or tap the microphone button to mute your microphone. Click or tap the button again to unmute your mic.

(11) Click or tap the camera button to turn off your camera. Click or tap the button again to turn the camera back on.

(12) When you're done talking, tap or click the red Disconnect button to end the call.

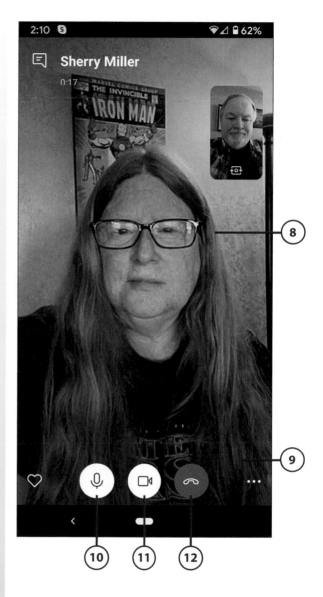

>>>*Go Further*

SPECIAL EFFECTS

Depending on your device, you may be able to add some special effects to your Skype chat sessions. Which special effects are available differs from device to device.

For example, if you're using Skype on a computer, you can "react" to a conversation by clicking the React button and selecting an emoji (crying face, surprised face, and so on). To choose a virtual background, click the More button and then select Choose Background Effect.

On an iPad or iPhone, you can "like" a conversation by tapping the heart icon. You can also "blur" your onscreen background by tapping the More (three-dot) icon and switching "on" Enable Background Blur. If you have an Android phone, no background effects are available, but you can still "like" the conversation by tapping the heart icon.

(It's more than likely that some or all of these effects will be rolled out across all devices eventually. Keep an eye out for them!)

Using Skype for Group Video Chats

Skype lets you participate in both one-on-one and group video chats. You can include up to 50 people in a group chat and even turn one-on-one chats into group chats.

Add Another Person to a Video Chat

The quickest way to create a group video chat is to add more people to an ongoing one-on-one call.

1. On a computer, click the Add People to the Call button.

2. From within an ongoing video chat in the mobile app, tap the More (three-dot) button; then select Add People.

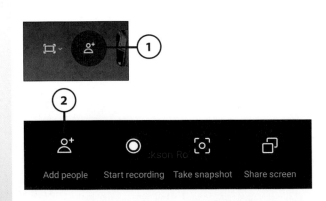

3 Search for or select the people you want to add.

4 Click Add.

5 The new person or persons are added to the video chat.

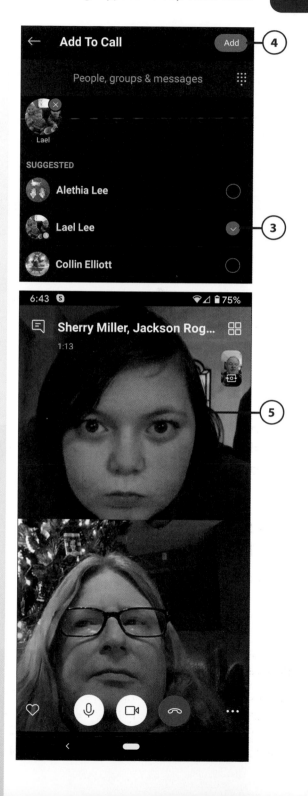

Start a New Group Chat

If you're hosting a larger group meeting, it's easier to invite all the participants up front. Here's how to do it:

(1) Select the Chats tab.

(2) On a computer, click New Chat and then select New Group Chat.

(3) In the mobile app, tap the New Chat icon.

(4) Tap New Group Chat.

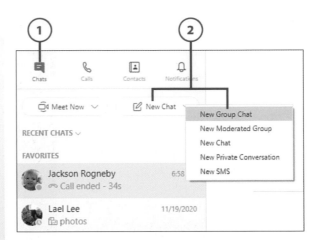

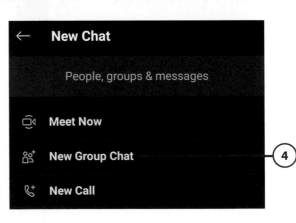

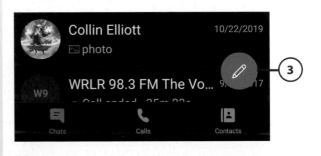

5. Enter a name for this group chat.

6. Click the next arrow.

7. Select the people you want to invite to your group chat.

8. Click or tap Done.

9. When the chat page appears, click or tap the Video Call button.

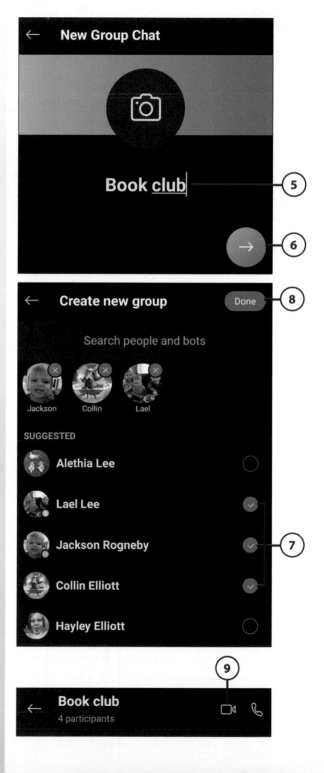

10 Skype notifies the other participants. When they arrive, they'll be
shown onscreen.

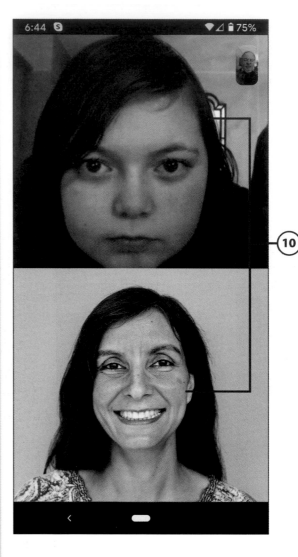

Participate in a Group Chat

There are several functions available in
Skype group video chats.

1 On a computer, to switch
between Grid View and Speaker
View, click the Switch View button and make a selection.

2 In the mobile app, to switch
between Grid View and Speaker
View, tap the Grid View/Speaker
View button.

3 To raise your hand during a meeting on a computer, click Raise Hand; in the mobile app, tap More (three-dots) and then tap Raise Hand.

4 To share your screen contents on a computer, click Share Screen; in the mobile app, tap More (three dots) and then tap Share Screen.

5 To choose the screen to share on a computer, select the window you want to share; on a mobile device, select the app you want to share. Then click or tap Start Sharing.

6 To exit the group chat, display the chat controls and tap or click End Call.

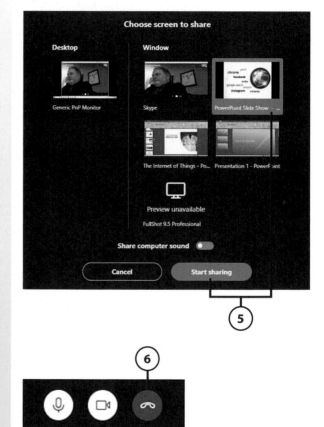

In this chapter, you learn how to use WhatsApp to video chat with friends and family on your phone.

→ Understanding WhatsApp
→ Video Chatting with WhatsApp

8

Using WhatsApp

WhatsApp is a video chat and text messaging platform that you may not be familiar with. It's popular globally, especially in South and Central America, India, China, Russia, and parts of Africa.

WhatsApp lets you chat one-on-one and in small groups from your iPhone or Android phone and is as easy to use as FaceTime is on Apple devices. You cannot, however, use WhatsApp for video chat on computers or tablets.

WhatsApp, like the other platforms covered in this book, is free to use.

Understanding WhatsApp

WhatsApp was founded in 2009 by two former Yahoo! employees, and the first version of the app, with text messaging only, was released that same year. The app was initially targeted at teens and young adults, although it has gained popularity among other users. By 2014, WhatsApp claimed more than 400 million active users around the world, and the company was subsequently purchased by Facebook.

Today, WhatsApp claims more than 2 billion users worldwide and has added voice calling video chats to its text messaging functionality.

One of WhatsApp's chief calling cards is the security of its communications. All WhatsApp messages—text, voice, and video—are end-to-end encrypted. This means that each message is scrambled (encrypted) at the source and not descrambled (decrypted) until it reaches the recipient. This provides an ultra-secure environment for all communications; even if a message is intercepted in transit, it can't be read or viewed because it's still encrypted.

Facebook Portal

WhatsApp, which is owned by Facebook, is also compatible with the Facebook Portal and Portal TV dedicated video chat devices. Learn more about Facebook Portal in Chapter 11, "Video Chatting with Facebook Portal, Amazon Echo Show, and Google Nest Hub Max."

Video Chatting with WhatsApp

To use WhatsApp for video chatting, you must first download and install the WhatsApp app on your mobile phone. You also need to create a WhatsApp account, for which you need to supply your phone number.

Answer a Video Call

Answering a video call on WhatsApp is just as easy as answering a normal phone call.

(1) When a calls comes through, you hear a sound and see a notification on your phone. Tap Answer or Accept. (Or, if you don't want to talk, tap Decline.)

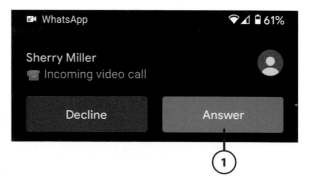

(2) You see the caller large on your screen. You see yourself in a smaller thumbnail.

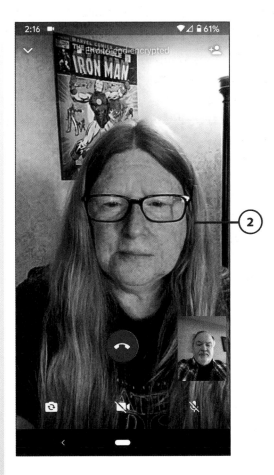

Make a Video Call

When you install the WhatsApp app and give it the necessary permissions, it accesses the existing contacts on your phone and recognizes those people who are also using WhatsApp. This makes it easy to make a video call to any of your connected contacts.

(1) From within the WhatsApp app, select the Calls tab to see recent calls.

(2) To call one of the people on the list, tap the Video Call (camera) icon for that person. Or...

(3) To call someone you've never called before, tap the New Call icon. The list of WhatsApp contacts on your phone displays. (This is the list only of your phone contacts who are also on WhatsApp.)

(4) Tap the Video Call (camera) icon for the person to whom you want to talk.

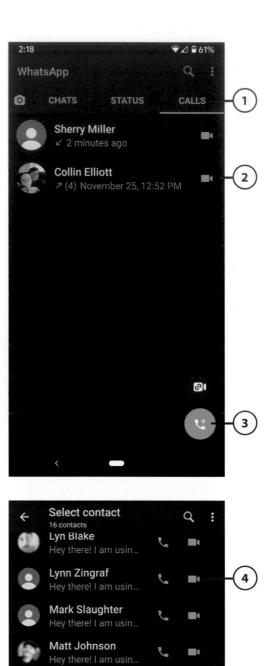

5. The person answering appears full-screen, and you appear in a smaller thumbnail.

6. Tap the screen to display the chat controls.

7. To mute your microphone, tap the microphone icon. Tap the icon again to unmute the mic.

8. To turn off your camera, tap the camera icon. Tap this icon again to turn your camera back on.

9. To end the call, tap the red End Call icon.

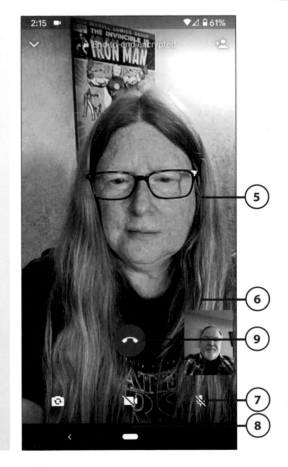

>>>Go Further
INVITING FRIENDS TO WHATSAPP

If you'd like your friends to join WhatsApp so you can chat with them, you can invite them to download the WhatsApp app.

From within the WhatsApp mobile app, go to the Calls tab and tap the New Call icon. Scroll to the very bottom of this page and then tap Invite Friends. Select your messaging or email program; then select the friend or friends you want to invite.

WhatsApp creates an invitation message you can send to those people. This message includes a link to download the WhatsApp mobile app. Read over and edit the message if you like; then tap Send to invite your friends to the WhatsApp family.

Call a Group

WhatsApp lets you make group video calls with up to eight participants. Here's how:

1. From within the WhatsApp app, select the Calls tab.

2. Tap the floating New Call icon.

3. Tap New Group Call.

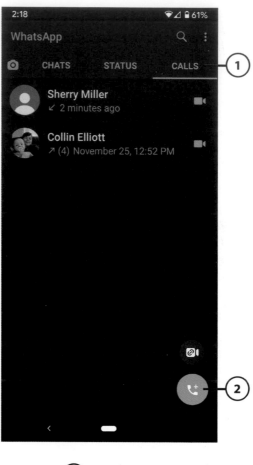

4 Tap to select the participants in this group call. You can add up to seven participants in addition to yourself.

5 Tap the Video Call (camera) icon to start the call. As people answer, their pictures will be added to the call screen.

5

← New group call
3 of 7 selected

Collin   Kyle   Mike

Abby Herzog

Chris White

Collin Elliott

D ck Carbone

D ew Shaman

K le Pederson

4

Add Other Participants to a Group Call

You can also add other participants to a video call in progress.

1 From within the video call, tap the Add Participants icon.

2 Tap the name of the new partici-pant you want to add and then tap Add. The new person is called and, if that person accepts, added to the call screen.

← Add Participant
16 contacts

Abby Herzog
Hey there! I am using WhatsApp.

Chris White

2

Collin Elliott
Hey there! I am using WhatsApp.

>>>Go Further

WHATSAPP AND MESSENGER ROOMS

WhatsApp limits chats to eight participants in its group chats. For larger chats, WhatsApp shifts you to Facebook Messenger Rooms (which makes sense, since Facebook owns WhatsApp). You can invite your WhatsApp contacts to a Messenger Room along with Facebook friends and anyone outside of WhatsApp or Facebook you decide to share the link with.

To open a Messenger Room from within the WhatsApp app, select the Calls tab and tap the floating Rooms (camera) icon. When prompted, tap Continue in Messenger, and then follow the onscreen instructions to open a Messenger Room.

Tap to switch to Messenger Rooms

Switching from WhatsApp to Facebook Messenger

Learn more about using Messenger Rooms in Chapter 6, "Using Facebook Messenger."

In this chapter, you learn how to video chat with Google's two video chat platforms: Google Duo and Google Meet.

→ Video Chatting with Google Duo
→ Video Meetings with Google Meet

9

Using Google Duo and Meet

Google is a key player in just about every technology sector, video chat included. Today Google offers two video chat platforms—Google Duo, targeted at consumers, and Google Meet, originally targeted at businesses but now with features that might appeal to people who hold larger video meetings. To use either Google Duo and Google Meet, you need a Gmail or other Google account.

Video Chatting with Google Duo

Google Duo is Google's current consumer-focused video chat platform. It's optimized for one-to-one video chat but can also handle group chats with up to 32 participants. Google Duo is free to use and has no time limitations on its meetings; all you—and anyone you're chatting with—need is a Google account and you're good to go.

If you're chatting on your phone or tablet, you connect via the Google Duo app. If you have an Android phone, chances are the app is already installed (because Google is the company behind the Android operating system). On many phones, Duo is completely integrated into your device, much like FaceTime is on Apple devices. Duo isn't limited to just Android devices, however; there is also a Duo app for iPhones and iPads. Look for the free app in your device's app store.

If you're using a Mac, Windows, or Chromebook computer, you use Duo from within your web browser. Just launch your browser and go to duo.google.com. You need to sign in with your Google account; then you see the Duo interface and can make and receive calls there. (If you don't yet have a Google account, you can sign up for one from the Duo sign-in page.)

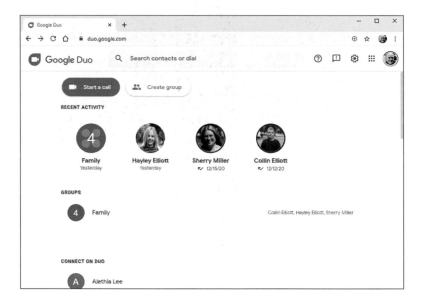

The Google Duo home screen (duo.google.com) in a web browser on a Windows computer

Accept a Duo Call

Accepting an invitation to video chat with Google Duo is slightly different on a phone than on other devices. These steps address both.

1 On your phone, when someone calls you to chat with Google Duo, your screen changes to the main Duo screen and displays the name of the person calling you. Swipe up to accept the call, or swipe down to decline.

2 On a tablet, when someone calls you, you see an onscreen notification. Tap or click the check mark to accept, or the red X to decline.

(3) If you're using Google Duo on a computer via the Duo website (in your web browser), you receive an onscreen notification.

(4) In your web browser, click Accept to accept the call or Decline to decline.

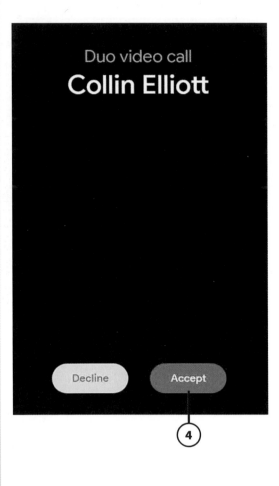

(5) You see the person calling you full screen, with your live thumbnail picture in a corner of the screen. On a phone or tablet, tap the screen to display the chat controls. (These controls are always present in the web version.)

(6) Tap or click the Mute Microphone button to mute your device's microphone. Tap or click this button again to unmute your mic.

(7) Tap or click the Turn Off Camera button to turn off your device's camera. Tap or click this button again to turn the camera back on.

(8) On a phone or tablet, tap the Switch button to switch between your device's front and rear cameras.

(9) On a phone or tablet, tap the main Effects or More (three-dot) button to access various screen effects.

(10) To blur the background on a phone or tablet, tap the Effects button and then tap Portrait.

(11) Tap the End Call button to end the call.

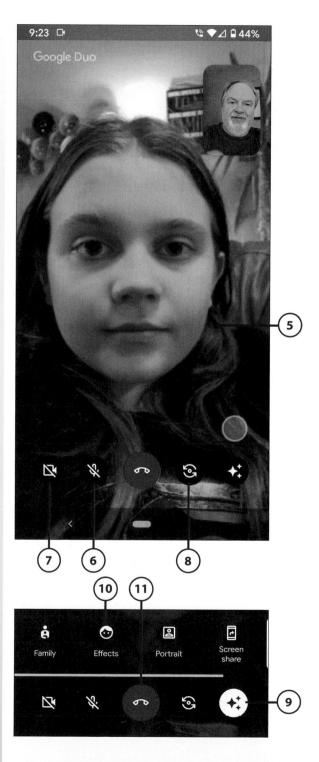

Make a Duo Call

To make a Duo call, you need to have the person you're calling in your Duo or phone contacts (if you're calling from your phone), or you need to know the person's email address or phone number.

(1) On a phone, swipe up from the bottom of the screen to display your favorite Duo contacts. On a tablet, these contacts are displayed in a panel on the right side of the screen. On the Duo website, the contacts are displayed on the Home screen. Tap to call one of these people. *Or...*

(2) Scroll further down to see contacts on your phone who also have Duo installed. Tap to call one of these people. *Or...*

Invite Others

On a phone or tablet, you can scroll even further down to view all your contacts who are not yet using Duo, with "Invite" next to their names. Tap a name to send an invitation to that person; if and when they accept, you can then call them.

(3) Start to enter a person's name, phone number, or email address directly into the Search Contacts or Dial (on a tablet, Search or Dial) field; then select the person you want from the results listed.

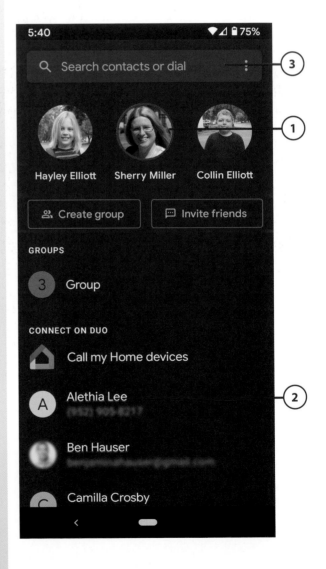

4 You see the person's contact
screen. Tap Video Call to initiate a
call.

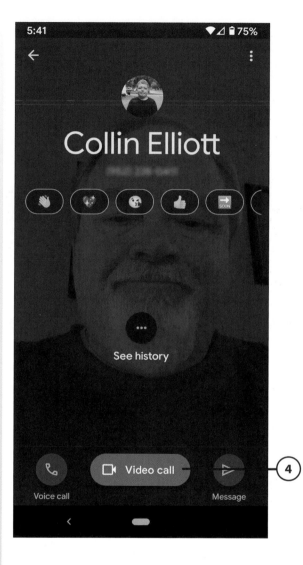

5 The person answering appears full screen, and your live picture is in a smaller thumbnail.

6 Tap or click End Call to end the call.

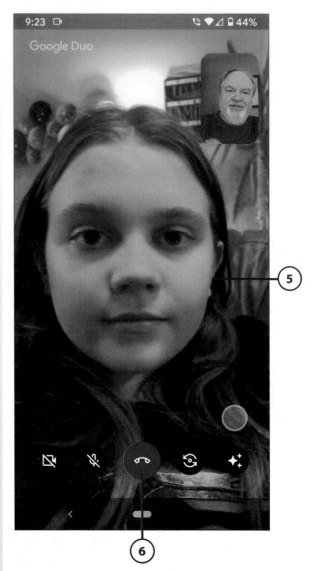

Create a Group Duo Call

Unlike some other video chat platforms, Google Duo doesn't let you add new people to an ongoing video chat. Instead, you need to start a group call with all desired participants invited from the start.

1 Tap or click Create Group.

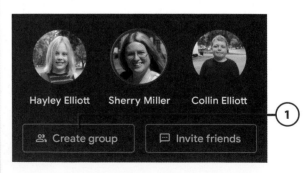

(2) If you see the Group panel, click Add People to proceed. (If you don't see this panel, skip this step and proceed directly to step 3.)

(3) From your Duo or phone contacts, select the people you want to include in this group chat.

(4) On a mobile device, tap Done; on a computer, click Add.

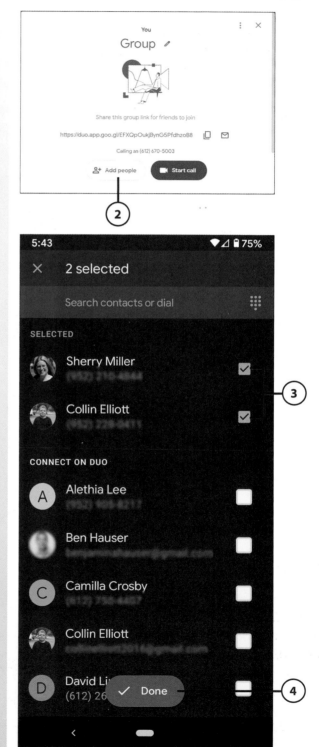

5 You see the Group screen or panel. Tap or click Start or Start Call to start the call.

6 If you've been invited to join a group Duo call, you see an onscreen invitation. Accept as normal.

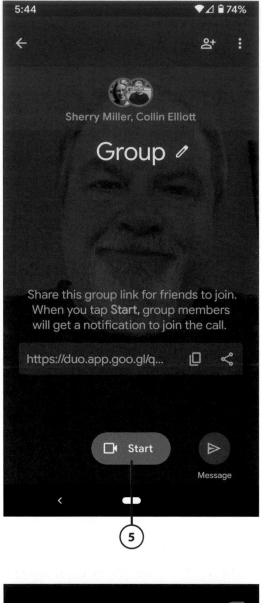

(**7**) You see all the participants in the call—everyone in their own pane.

(**8**) Display the chat controls (if necessary)

(**9**) To end or leave the call, tap or click End Call (if you're the host) or Leave Call (if you're a participant).

Video Meetings with Google Meet

Google Meet is Google's other video chat platform. Although you can chat one on one with Google Meet, it's really designed for larger video meetings of up to 100 participants. All participants need Google accounts, which anyone using Gmail or any other Google service already has.

The consumer version of Meet is free but has a 60-minute time limit for all meetings. Google offers paid versions of Meet, targeted at businesses, that offer longer time limits.

Like Google Duo, Google Meet is available for all devices and platforms, including Android and iOS phones and tablets; download the free Meet app from your device's app store. On a Chromebook, Mac, or Windows computer, you access Google Meet via the service's website at meet.google.com.

Accept a Google Meet Invitation

When someone invites you to a Google Meet meeting, you receive an invitation via email.

1. From within the email, tap or click the Join Meeting link or button.

2. You see the Join screen in the Google Meet app or, if you're on your computer, in your web browser. Tap or click Join, Join Now, or Ask to Join, depending on your device.

3. All participants appear onscreen. On a phone, you appear in a smaller live thumbnail. On other devices, you appear in your own pane. If necessary, tap or mouse over the screen to display the chat controls.

4. Tap or click the Turn Off Microphone button to mute your device's microphone. Tap or click this button again to unmute your mic.

5. Tap or click the Turn Off Camera button to turn off your device's camera. Tap or click this button again to turn the camera back on.

6. Tap or click the End Call button to leave the meeting.

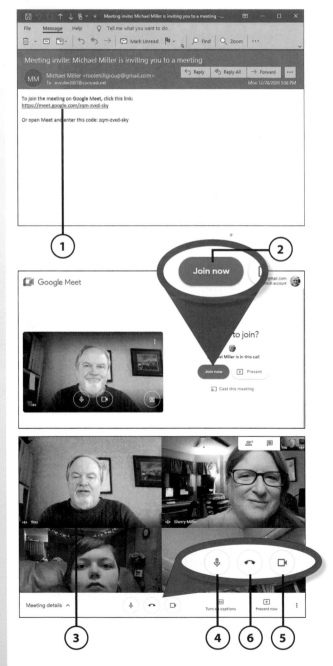

Host an Instant Meeting on a Computer

Google Meet enables you to host a meeting that starts immediately (called an instant meeting) or schedule a meeting to start later. This task explains how to use your computer to host an instant meeting.

(1) From the meet.google.com website, click New Meeting.

(2) Click Start an Instant Meeting.

(3) Click Join Now.

(4) You are in the meeting by yourself. In the Add Others panel, click Add People. (If you don't see the Add Others panel, click Show Everyone the Meeting Details pane.)

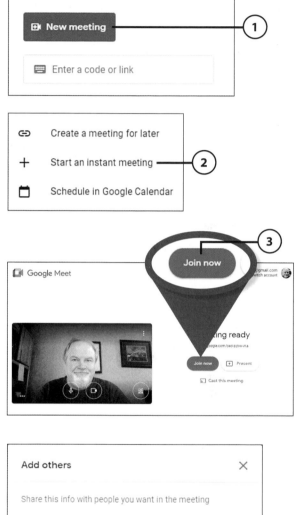

5. Select or enter the names or emails for the people you want to invite.

6. Click Send Email, and those people receive an invitation via email. When they click the link in the invitation, they are admitted to the meeting.

7. All participants appear onscreen. Mouse over the screen to display the chat controls.

8. Click Leave Call to leave the call. The meeting continues until the last person leaves.

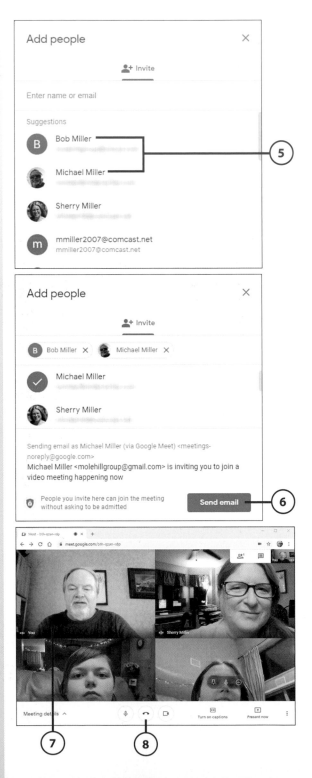

Host an Instant Meeting on a Phone

Hosting an instant meeting from the Google Meet app on your phone is a little different, mainly in how you invite others to join.

1. From within the Google Meet app, tap New Meeting.

2. Tap Start an Instant Meeting.

3. Your meeting starts with you as the only attendee. Tap Share Invite to display your device's Share screen.

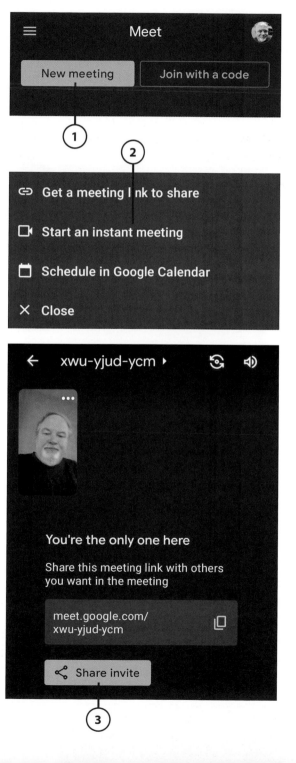

④ Select how you want to share the invitation (email, messaging, and such) and then select who you want to send it to. When people receive your invitation and click the link, they are admitted to the meeting.

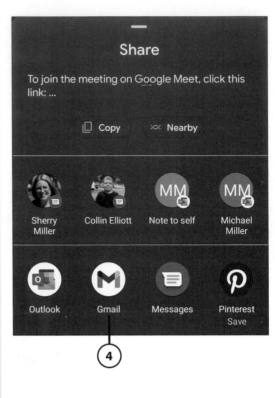

(5) As participants join the meeting, they appear onscreen. The current speaker appears in the main pane, and other participants appear as live thumbnails. Tap the screen to display the chat controls.

(6) Tap Leave Call to leave the call. The meeting continues until the last person leaves.

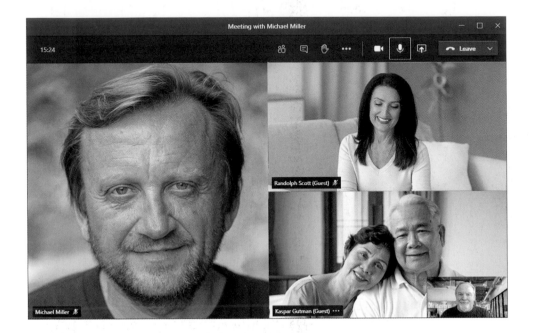

In this chapter, you learn how to video chat with Microsoft Teams.

→ Understanding Microsoft Teams
→ Video Chatting with Microsoft Teams

10

Using Microsoft Teams

Microsoft Teams is a full-featured collaborative communication platform, originally targeted at businesses, that includes a robust video meeting component. During the COVID-19 crisis, Microsoft revamped Teams' video chat to be more user-friendly and appealing to individual consumers—and to be more competitive with Zoom.

Understanding Microsoft Teams

As I mention in Chapter 7, "Using Skype," Microsoft already has a video chat platform called Skype. It's been around for decades and is popular with both consumers and businesses.

Microsoft Teams is a much different beast. Microsoft initially designed Teams to be a full-service communication platform for business collaboration. It offers a number of ways for business employees to communicate with each other, of which video chat is just one component.

Microsoft Teams is part of the Microsoft 365 suite of applications. Microsoft offers Teams to businesses and other organizations on a subscription basis, ranging from $5 to $20 per user per month. (That's typically how this type of business software is marketed.)

This book focuses on a free version of Teams that Microsoft offers to individuals. The free version of Teams is a new thing, inspired by the rise in video chatting due to the COVID-19 crisis. This version allows group meetings with up to 300 participants; chats can last all day, free of charge.

To host a Teams meeting, you need to sign in with a Microsoft account, although participants do not need a Microsoft account to join meetings started by others. You can use Teams on any computer via the Google Chrome and Microsoft Edge web browsers or the Teams desktop app. Teams apps are also available for Android and iOS phones and tablets.

Video Chat and More

The full Microsoft Teams platform includes features such as one-on-one and group chats, file sharing, voice and video calling and conferencing, live events, and more. This chapter covers only video chatting; there's a lot more to Teams that isn't relevant to this book. You can learn more about Microsoft Teams at www.microsoft.com/en-us/microsoft-365/microsoft-teams/.

Video Chatting with Microsoft Teams

Microsoft Teams isn't difficult to use, although its interface isn't quite as consumer-friendly as competing chat platforms. It's probably not most people's first choice for a simple one-on-one video chat platform but is a viable alternative to Zoom and Google Meet for group video meetings.

Given that Teams is optimized for larger team meetings, I'm showing you how to use Teams for group meetings in your computer's web browser. You can also use Teams on your phone or tablet, using the (free) Teams app; operation on those devices is similar.

Browsers

Microsoft Teams works with the Google Chrome and Microsoft Edge browsers, but not with Apple's Safari. If you're using a Mac, you'll need to install Chrome to use Teams.

Accept an Invitation

When someone launches a Teams meeting, you receive an invitation via email.

(1) From within the invitation email, click the link. This opens or switches to your web browser.

(2) Click Continue on This Browser, which takes you to the Microsoft Teams website. (You also have the option of joining from the Teams app if you have it, but you don't need the app to use Teams.) You go to the Microsoft Teams website.

(3) If prompted, click Allow to let Teams use your microphone and camera; then click Join Now.

(4) You are now placed in a waiting room (called the Lobby) until the host admits you to the meeting.

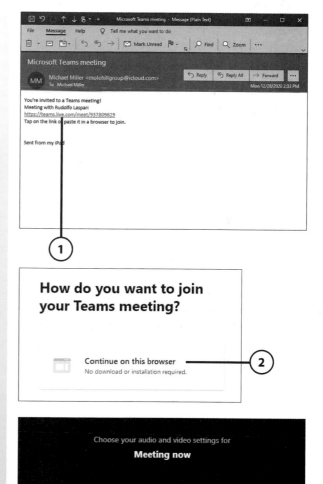

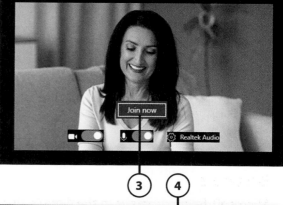

5 Once in the meeting, if you're using the web version of Teams, you see the current speaker onscreen, yourself in a live thumbnail, and icons for the other speakers at the bottom of the screen. (If you're using the desktop app, you see all the speakers in a grid.) If necessary, mouse over or click the screen to display the chat controls.

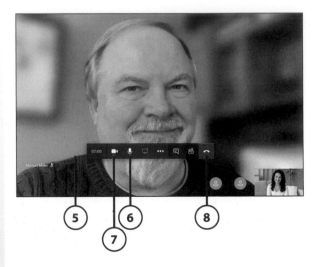

6 Click the Mute button to mute your microphone. Click the button again to unmute your mic.

7 Click the Turn Camera Off button to turn off your camera. Click this button again to turn your camera back on.

8 Click the Hang Up button to leave the meeting.

Launch a Teams Meeting

To host a Microsoft Teams meeting, you need to have a Microsoft account (it's free, and you already have one if you have an Outlook or Hotmail email address). When you're hosting, it's easiest to use the Microsoft Teams desktop app, which you can download from www.microsoft.com/en-us/microsoft-365/microsoft-teams/download-app. These steps assume you're using the desktop app.

1 Open the Microsoft Teams desktop app and click to select the Chat tab.

2 Click New Meeting icon.

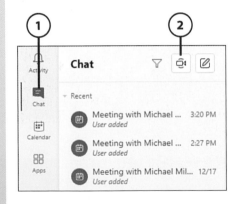

(**3**) Accept or edit the meeting name.

(**4**) Click Start Meeting.

(**5**) Make sure you have your microphone and camera turned on; then click Join Now.

(**6**) The meeting starts with you as the only participant and the Invite People to Join You window displayed. Click which email option you want to use to send invitations.

Meeting name   ×

Meeting with Michael Miller ——————— **3**

Get a link to share

Start meeting ——— **4**

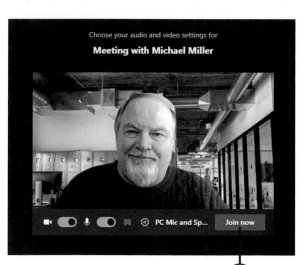

Choose your audio and video settings for
Meeting with Michael Miller

PC Mic and Sp...   Join now

5

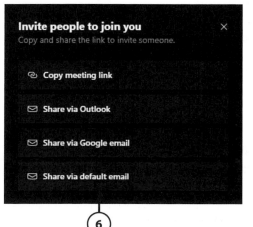

Invite people to join you   ×
Copy and share the link to invite someone.

        ⊘ **Copy meeting link**

        ✉ **Share via Outlook**

        ✉ **Share via Google email**

        ✉ **Share via default email**

6

(7) The selected email program opens with the invitation text and link already filled in. Edit the text if you like.

(8) Enter the email addresses of the people you want to invite to the meeting.

(9) Click Send.

(10) Close the Invite People to Join You window.

(11) When people join the meeting, they're placed in the virtual Lobby, and you see an onscreen message. Click Admit to let them into the meeting.

(12) You see the other people in your meeting. Your live picture appears in a thumbnail in the corner.

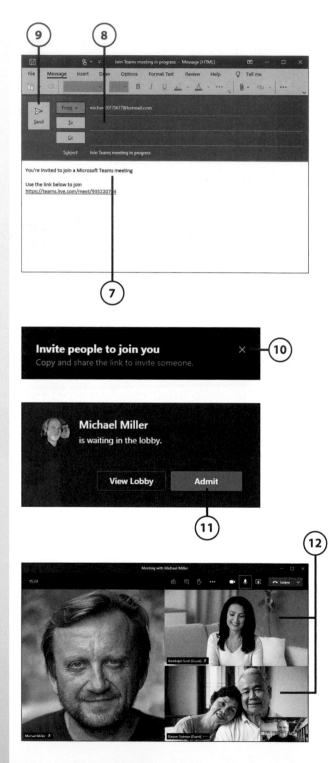

13 Click the Leave button to leave the meeting. *Or...*

14 Click the down arrow next to the Leave button and then click End Meeting to end the meeting for all participants.

15 If prompted to end the meeting for everyone, click End.

13

Leave

14

End the meeting?

You'll end the meeting for everyone.

Cancel   End   **15**

>>>*Go Further*

SCHEDULING A MEETING IN ADVANCE

The free version of Microsoft Teams lets you schedule video meetings in advance. From the Teams desktop app, click the Calendar tab and then click the New Meeting button at the top of the calendar. Enter a title for the meeting, select a start and end time, enter details about the meeting, and then click Save.

You're asked how you want to share the meeting; the easiest way to proceed is to click Copy Link. You can email the people you want to invite and paste the link to the meeting into the email message. When the start time approaches, open the Teams app and join the meeting.

In this chapter, you learn to video chat with smart displays such as the Facebook Portal, Amazon Echo Show, and Google Nest Hub Max.

→ Chatting with Facebook Portal

→ Chatting with Amazon Echo Show

→ Chatting with Google Nest Hub Max

Video Chatting with Facebook Portal, Amazon Echo Show, and Google Nest Hub Max

Most people video chat with their phones, tablets, and computers. There is a new category of device, however, that makes video chat quite easy. These devices are called *smart displays*.

These standalone smart displays feature a touchscreen display, speaker(s), camera, and microphone—everything you need for a video chat session. You can use these devices by tapping the touchscreen or using voice commands. What makes these smart displays especially easy to use for video chats is that, once you set them up, you can use voice commands, which makes them particularly attractive to people who aren't tech savvy. These smart displays also feature a touchscreen display, speaker(s), camera, and microphone—everything you need for a video chat session.

There are three primary manufacturers of smart displays today—Facebook, with its line of Facebook Portal devices; Amazon, with its Echo Show devices; and Google, with its Nest Hub Max device. All these devices do similar things but in somewhat different ways.

Chatting with Facebook Portal

We'll start this chapter by looking at the Facebook Portal because it's the only dedicated video chat device and the most popular. Facebook Portal lets users easily video chat with their Facebook friends via Facebook Messenger, with no confusing buttons to push or menus to click.

In addition to the core video chat functionality, all Portal models also have Amazon's Alexa virtual assistant built in, so you can easily control the devices using voice commands. You can also control the device using the touchscreen. The Portal packs some pretty cool features to make your chats more interesting, such as camera tracking and an interactive Story Time for use with younger family members.

Understanding Facebook Portal

Unlike the Amazon and Google devices discussed later in this chapter, the Facebook Portal is designed with video chat as its primary function. It includes a touchscreen display, microphone, speakers, and camera in one self-contained device.

The Facebook Portal Mini smart display

It Does a Little Bit More

In addition to video chatting, the Facebook Portal does a few other minor things, such as serving as a digital picture frame, letting family members leave notes for one another onscreen, and playing music from Pandora and Spotify. Those functions aside, the Facebook Portal designed primarily for video chatting, unlike the other devices covered in this chapter.

Portal devices come in three sizes, as well as a Portal TV variation that doesn't have a screen and connects to any TV for its display. All Facebook Portal models let users video chat using Facebook Messenger, Messenger Rooms (for larger group chats), or WhatsApp. (WhatsApp is owned by Facebook.) The Portal also is compatible with several business-oriented chat services, such as BlueJeans, GoToMeeting, Webex, and Workplace. In addition, you can use the Portal (but not Portal TV) to video chat via Zoom. You cannot, however, use a Portal to chat via Apple FaceTime, Google Duo, Skype, or other chat platforms.

The Portal is easy to set up and easy to use—initiating a video chat is as easy as tapping a person's picture on the Portal screen or telling Portal to call a person, and answering a video call is even easier. It's no wonder that so many people are buying Portal devices for their older or less-technical relatives.

>>>*Go Further*

ONCE A FLOP, NOW A HIT: THE FALL AND RISE OF FACEBOOK PORTAL

When the first Facebook Portal device was released in 2018, it was not an immediate success. Critics and consumers alike bemoaned the fact that it didn't do much more than video chat, even though it did that very well. In fact, many in the industry considered it a flop.

When the COVID crisis hit, forcing people to quarantine in their homes, Portal sales saw a sudden and dramatic resurgence. With video chatting now the only way to stay in touch with socially distanced relatives, Portal's limited functionality and simple operation proved to be a real plus. Many families set up their less-technical parents or grandparents with a Portal device to stay in touch.

Experts say that Facebook Portal is especially popular with people aged 65 and up. These people like the Portal because it's easy to use with no confusing buttons to push or menus to click.

This newfound popularity is echoed in Facebook's sales numbers. In May 2020, Facebook CEO Mark Zuckerberg reported that Portal sales grew by more than 10 times what they were before the COVID crisis. Apparently, it just took a little time for the Portal to find its place in our homes.

Choosing a Facebook Portal Model

Facebook currently makes three models of the Portal smart display, along with a model without a screen that connects to your TV. The differences are mainly in the screen size and the camera:

- **Portal:** This is the standard smart display with a 10" HD display. It sells for $179.

- **Portal Mini:** This is a slightly smaller version than the regular portal, with an 8" HD display. It sells for $129.

- **Portal+:** This version has a large 15.6" HD display, sturdy stand with rotating screen, and multiple speakers. It sells for $279.

- **Portal TV:** This is a small device that includes a camera, microphone, and remote control. It connects to any TV via HDMI so you can view and hear your video chats on the larger TV screen and through its speakers; think of it as a (large) webcam for your living room TV. It sells for $149.

The Facebook Portal TV, which displays on your television

Table 11.1 compares these models.

Table 11.1   Facebook Portal Models

Model	Screen Size	Camera	Speakers	Price
Portal Mini	8"	13 MP (megapixel), 114-degree field of view	2 front-firing speakers plus rear woofer	$129
Portal	10"	13 MP, 114-degree field of view	2 front-firing speakers and rear woofer	$179
Portal+	15.6"	12.5 MP, 140-degree field of view	2 2" tweeters and a 4" woofer	$279
Portal TV	N/A	12.5 MP, 120-degree field of view	N/A	$149

Comparing Cameras

When comparing the picture quality of cameras, look at two factors: resolution, measured in megapixels (MPs), and field of view. When it comes to resolution, the more megapixels, the sharper the picture. The field of view measures the width of the field that the camera lens sees; the larger the field of view, in degrees, the more you see, left to right.

Among the three freestanding Portal models, the main difference is screen size. All Portal models have a relatively wide field of view (114 degrees on the Portal and Portal Mini, 140 degrees on the Portal+). All Portals use special camera-tracking technology that helps the camera keep its focus on you as you move around the room. In addition, the built-in camera automatically zooms out if you move away from the device (or if you have multiple people huddled together to chat as a group) and zooms back in when you get closer.

Learn more about the different Facebook Portal models at portal.facebook.com.

Using the Facebook Portal

When you unbox and plug in your Portal, you walk through a simple step-by-step installation and configuration procedure. Essentially, you connect the Portal to your home Wi-Fi network and your Facebook or WhatsApp account. (Most people use Portal with Facebook.)

You can set up the Portal to display in either landscape (horizontal) or portrait (vertical) orientations. Just turn it sidewise to move from one orientation to another. If you mostly talk to people using Messenger on their phones, portrait orientation is best; if you talk to people on their computers, landscape orientation is the way to go.

Facebook Portal in portrait mode

There are a few physical controls on the Portal itself: volume up and volume down buttons and a three-way switch that lets you do the following:

- Physically cover the camera and mute the microphone
- Physically cover the camera without muting the microphone
- Continue normal camera and microphone operation

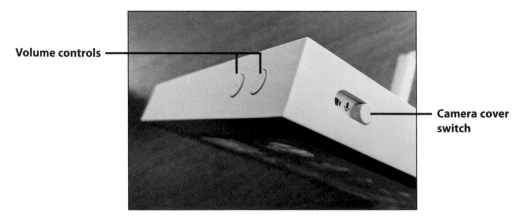

Facebook Portal's physical controls

You can control the Portal with Alexa voice commands by first saying, "Hey Portal," and then issuing a command. For example, to start a video call, say, "Hey Portal, call Bob Smith." You can also control the device via the touchscreen.

It's Not All Good

Privacy Concerns

Facebook has a checkered history in terms of user privacy. Over the years, the company allowed third-party apps to access private user data, tracked user activity outside of Facebook, and enabled controversial facial recognition technology, among other things.

Facebook's ongoing privacy issues makes some people wary of putting a camera directly connected to Facebook in their living room or bedroom. Fortunately, the Portal has a switch in the top-right corner that, when engaged, physically covers the device's camera so Facebook can't easily spy on you. (Learn more about these and other privacy concerns in Chapter 15, "Staying Safe While Video Chatting.")

Change Portal Settings

You can change the settings on your Portal at any time.

1. Tap the screen to go to the Home screen.

2. Swipe from right to left to go to the next screen, then swipe again until you see the Settings tile.

(3) Tap Settings.

(4) Tap the General tab to configure device settings, call settings,
and sound, such as Portal name,
Wi-Fi network, city, and alarm
volume—all of which are automatically set but you can change
if you like.

(5) Tap the Display tab to configure
what shows on the screen, such
as Facebook photos, birthdays,
and tips. You also use this tab to
set the screen brightness.

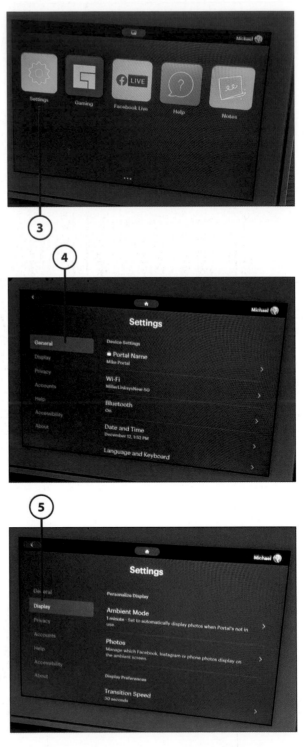

6. Tap the Privacy tab to view and configure various privacy-related settings. (In most instances, the default settings are fine.)

7. Tap the Accounts tab to switch to a different Facebook account and connect to your Alexa, Pandora, and Spotify accounts.

8. Tap the Accessibility tab to make the screen easier to see.

Help and About

The Help tab tells you where to get help with your Portal. The About tab displays device and system information.

Configure Your Favorite Contacts

Your Portal can call any person on your Facebook friends list. Instead of scrolling through the entire list every time you want to make a call, however, it's easier to designate the people you call most often as favorites. You can then tap a favorite's name or picture on the Portal Home screen to initiate a video chat.

You are asked to select some of your favorites during the initial Portal setup. You can add more favorites at any time.

1. Tap the screen to go to the Home screen.

2. Scroll to the bottom of the screen and tap Add Favorites.

3. Scroll through your list of Facebook friends and tap to select the ones you want to add as favorites. (You can also deselect people to remove them from your favorites list.)

4. Tap Add when done.

Accept a Portal Call

If you have a Portal, any of your Facebook friends can call you for a video chat. Here's how you answer the call.

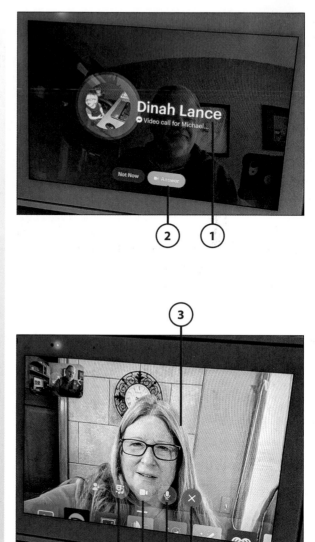

1. When someone calls you, your Portal chimes and the screen changes to notify you of the call and display the name of the person calling.

2. Tap Answer to answer the call and start chatting. (You can also tap Not Now if you don't want to chat.) Alternatively, you can say, "Hey Portal, answer."

3. The other person appears on the main screen; your picture is in a smaller thumbnail. Tap the screen to show the chat controls.

4. Tap the Mute Microphone button to mute your microphone's sound. Tap this button again to unmute the mic.

5. Tap the Turn Off Video (camera) button to turn off your Portal's camera. Tap this button again to turn the camera back on.

6. Tap the Effects button to apply various special effects and filters.

7. Tap the red End Call button to end the call. Alternatively, say, "Hey Portal, hang up."

Make a Portal Call

You can call any of your Facebook friends or WhatsApp contacts by tapping that person's name/picture on the Portal Home screen or using voice commands.

(1) Tap the screen to go to the Home screen.

(2) People with whom you've recently chatted are shown at the top of the screen. Tap a person to call them again. *Or…*

(3) Scroll down to view your favorites. Tap any favorite to initiate a call. (You see a green dot by the names of people who are currently online.) *Or…*

(4) To call a contact who is not yet on your favorites list, tap All Contacts or Contacts and Rooms.

(5) Tap the name of the person you want to chat with.

(6) Tap Video to initiate the call. *Or…*

7. From any Portal screen, say, "Hey Portal, call *contact*" (substituting the person's name for *contact*). So, for example, I wanted to call Dinah Lance, so I said, "Hey Portal, call Dinah Lance."

8. When the person you're calling answers, that person's image appears on the main screen; your picture is in a smaller thumbnail. Tap the screen to show and use the chat controls.

9. Tap End Call or say, "Hey Portal, hang up" to end the chat.

Participate in a Messenger Room

In addition to one-on-one chatting, Portal lets you participate in group chats in Messenger Rooms.

1. If you receive an invitation to join a Room, typically via a normal Facebook message, that invitation should include a link. From the Portal Home screen, tap All Contacts or Contacts and Rooms, select the Rooms tab, and then tap Join Room with a Link and enter that link. You're ushered into the Room.

2. To create your own Room, go to the Rooms screen and tap Create Room and follow the onscreen instructions.

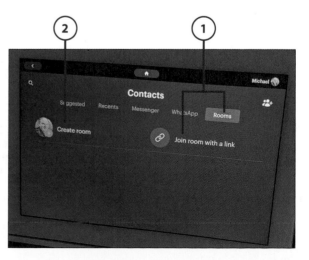

Messenger Rooms

Learn more about Messenger Rooms in Chapter 6, "Using Facebook Messenger."

>>>Go Further

BE THE STORY WITH STORY TIME

If you're chatting with younger members of your family, you may want to take advantage of the Portal's unique Story Time feature. Story Time lets you read one of the Portal's short picture books to any kids on the other end of the line as it inserts your live picture into the story's onscreen graphics.

Reading a Story Time story

To use Story Time, start a video chat as normal, display the chat controls, tap the Effects button, and then tap Story Time. Tap to select a story and then tap Play. Read the text as it appears onscreen.

Portal comes with a library of Story Time stories, including titles from Dr. Seuss and books about Pete the Cat and Llama Llama. More free stories are added on a regular basis.

Chatting with Amazon Echo Show

You may be familiar with the Amazon Echo smart speaker and accompanying Alexa intelligent assistant. You may even have an Echo or Echo Dot in your home. These devices respond to your voice commands and let you look up information, control smart home devices, and more.

Amazon's Echo and Echo Dot devices are speakers only; they don't have screens. Amazon does, however, make several Echo Show devices that combine Echo functionality with a touchscreen display. An Echo Show not only displays the information you ask about but—more relevant to this discussion—lets you video chat with other Echo Show users.

Echo Show Does More

Like all Amazon Echo devices, the Echo Show offers a lot of functionality. This chapter covers only the video chat function.

How Video Chatting Works with Echo Show

You can use any Echo Show device to video chat with other friends and family who also have Echo Show devices. If a friend or family member has an Echo Show and you don't, you can use the Amazon Alexa app on your phone to video chat with them—no Echo Show required on your end.

This last option is a good one if you're chatting with an older or less-technical family member. Set them up with an Echo Show, make sure it's connected to the person's own Amazon account, and then use the Alexa app on your phone to video chat with them. It's pretty easy.

Note that when you're video chatting with an Echo Show, it's strictly an Amazon thing. You can't use your Echo Show to chat on FaceTime, Skype, Zoom, or other video chat platforms.

Choosing an Amazon Echo Show Model

Amazon currently offers three different versions of the Echo Show in three different screen sizes:

- **Echo Show 5:** This model has a 5.5-inch screen and sells for $89.99.
- **Echo Show 8:** This model has an 8-inch screen and sells for $129.99.
- **Echo Show 10:** This model has a large 10.1-inch screen and sells for $249.99.

The Amazon Echo Show 5 smart display

All three models have similar functionality and operate in the same fashion. The Echo Show 10 is a little different in that the display is on a base that automatically swivels left and right to keep you in the camera shot as you move about the room. It also has a considerably better camera and better sound.

Table 11.2 details the features of each model.

Table 11.2   Echo Show Models

Model	Screen Size	Camera	Speakers	Price
Echo Show 5	5.5"	1 MP	1 (1.7")	$89.99
Echo Show 8	8"	1 MP	2 (2")	$129.99
Echo Show 10	10.1"	13 MP	2 (1") tweeters and 1 (3") woofer	$249.99

Learn more about the various Echo Show models at www.amazon.com.

Answer a Video Call

When someone wants to initiate a video chat, your Echo Show issues a chime and voice notification. You also see the person's name onscreen, as well as a dimmed image from your Echo Show's camera.

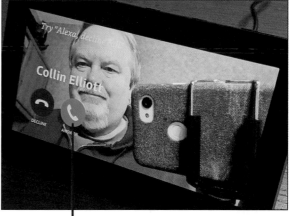

1. When you receive notification of an incoming video call, tap the green Answer button. (Tap Decline if you don't want to answer the call.) *Or…*

2. Say, "Alexa, answer the call." (Not shown.)

3. The image of the person calling fills the Echo Show screen, while your picture appears in a smaller thumbnail.

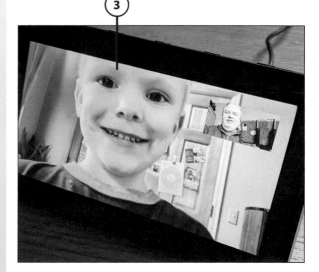

4 To raise or lower the call's volume, press the volume up and down buttons on the top of the Echo Show device. (You can also say, "Alexa, turn up the volume" or "Alexa, turn down the volume.")

5 Tap the Echo Show screen to view other chat controls.

6 Tap Mute to mute your microphone. Tap this button again to unmute your mic. (You can also say, "Alexa, mute" or "Alexa, unmute.")

7 Tap Video Off to turn off the camera. Tap this button again to turn the camera back on. (You can also say, "Alexa, turn off the camera" or "Alexa, turn on the camera.")

8 Tap End to end the call or say, "Alexa, hang up."

Video Call Another Echo Show

You can initiate a video chat with another Echo Show user using either the device's touchscreen or your voice. You set up other Echo devices as contacts from within the Alexa app on your mobile device.

1 The easiest way to initiate a video chat is by voice. Say, "Alexa, video call *contact*," where *contact* is the name of the contact. In this example, you would call Collin Elliott by saying, "Alexa, video call Collin Elliott." Alexa may ask you to confirm the contact before making the call. *Or...*

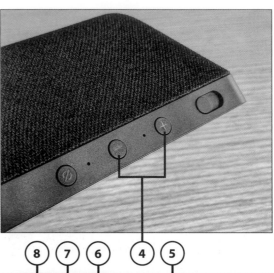

(2) Swipe the Echo Show display from right to left to open the feature menu.

(3) Tap Communicate.

(4) Tap Show Contacts to display your contact list.

(5) Scroll down and tap All Contacts to display all your contacts.

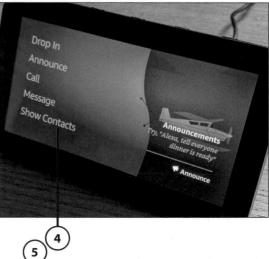

6 Tap the contact you want to chat with. This opens the contact's information screen.

7 Tap the Call icon

8 When the person you're calling answers, his or her picture fills up the Echo Show screen. Your picture appears in a smaller thumbnail.

9 Tap the screen and then tap End (or say, "Alexa, hang up") to end the call.

>>>*Go Further*

VIRTUAL CAREGIVING WITH THE ALEXA CARE HUB

If you are a caregiver for someone but you can't always be there in person, consider using Amazon's Alexa Care Hub. This is a service that lets you check in or monitor the other person's well-being from your mobile phone or tablet. The person you're monitoring needs an Amazon Echo device (the Echo Show, with its video function, is best, but a regular Echo or Echo Dot also works), and you need the Amazon Alexa app on your phone or tablet.

You can configure the Alexa Care Hub to send you alerts when the other Echo device is first used in the morning, or if it's not used by a certain time. The Echo device monitors activity by category, and you view that data through a feed on the Alexa app.

The Alexa Care Hub also includes an emergency function. To activate this function, your loved one would say, "Alexa, call for help." Echo then calls, texts, and sends a push notification to you. You can also use Alexa's drop-in (or, on an Echo Show, video chat) function to check in on your loved one at any time.

To learn more about the Alexa Care Hub, which is free, go to www.amazon.com/carehub.

Chatting with Google Nest Hub Max

The Google Nest Hub Max is another smart display that you can use for video chatting. It's a large display that lets you video chat one on one with Google Duo or participate in group video meetings with Google Meet. It also incorporates the Google Assistant intelligent assistant, which lets you control everything with voice commands (always starting with "Hey Google").

Get to Know the Google Nest Hub Max

Unlike Facebook and Amazon, which offer multiple models of their Portal and Echo Show devices, Google offers only a single Google Nest Hub Max. It has a 10" HD touchscreen display, 6.5 MP camera with 127-degree field of view, two 0.7" tweeters, one 3" woofer, and a built-in microphone array, and sells for $229.

The Google Nest Hub Max smart display

More Than Chat

The Google Nest Hub Max is more than just a video chat device. You can use it to watch YouTube and Netflix videos, as well as listen to your favorite music via Pandora, Spotify, and YouTube Music. It also interfaces with a variety of smart home devices, including Google's popular Nest Thermostat and Nest Cam security cameras. As noted, the Google Nest Hub Max can do a lot more than just video chat. For the purpose of this book, however, I'm focusing solely on the Nest Hub Max's video chat features.

Accept a Google Duo Call

The Nest Hub Max uses Google Duo for its one-on-one video chats. You can chat from the Nest Hub Max to any device using Google Duo, including smart-phones, tablets, and computers.

Zoom Calls

As this book is being written, Google announced that it would be adding Zoom capability to the Nest Hub Max. Check Google's website for the availability of this feature and instructions on how to use it.

1. When someone calls you, the Nest Hub Max announces the call, plays a notification sound, and displays the name of the person calling. Tap Accept to accept the call. (You can also tap Decline if you don't want to take the call.) Alternatively, say, "Hey Google, answer."

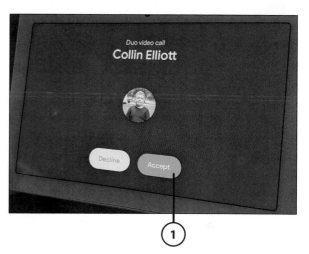

2. The person calling you fills the entire screen. You appear in a smaller thumbnail. Tap the screen to display the chat controls.

3. Tap the Mute button to mute the microphone. Tap this button again to unmute the mic. (You can also say, "Hey Google, mute" or "Hey Google, unmute.")

4. Tap the Camera button to turn off the camera. Tap this button again to turn the camera back on. (You can also say, "Hey Google, turn the camera off" or "Hey Google, turn the camera on.")

5. By default, the device's camera follows you as you move and zooms in or out as necessary. To turn off this feature, tap the Follow Person button. Tap this button again to turn the follow feature back on.

6. Tap the red End Call button, or say, "Hey Google, hang up," to end the current call.

Make a Google Duo Call

You can also use the Google Nest Hub Max to make new video calls to any of your Google Duo contacts. You do it all with Google Assistant voice commands.

1 Say, "Hey Google, video call *contact*," where *contact* is the Duo contact with whom you want to chat.

2 When the other person answers, their picture fills up the entire screen, and your picture appears in a smaller thumbnail. Tap the screen to display the chat controls.

3 Tap the red End Call button to end the call.

Google Duo and Google Meet

Learn more about Google's video chat services in Chapter 9, "Using Google Duo and Meet."

Participate in a Google Meet Meeting

In addition to one-on-one Google Duo video chats, you can also use the Nest Hub Max to participate in group video meetings via Google Meet.

1. When it's time for the meeting to begin, say, "Hey Google, join a meeting." (Not shown.)

2. You should have received a meeting code via email when the meeting was scheduled. Enter that code.

3. Tap the right arrow. You'll be admitted to the group video meeting.

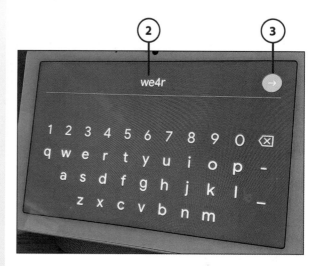

Creating a Video Meeting

You can also use your Nest Hub Max to create a new video meeting with Google Meet, although it's a bit more complicated. Start by saying, "Hey Google, start a meeting." This opens a new meeting and sends a note to the Google Assistant app on your phone. You have to use the mobile app to invite others to the meeting; you can't do it from the Nest Hub Max.

In this chapter, you get advice on how to look and sound better in your video chats.

→ Creating the Right Environment
→ Making a Better Connection
→ Improving Your Appearance
→ Preparing for a Video Meeting

12

Tips and Tricks for Better Video Chats

Have you ever seen someone in a video chat dressed in pajamas? Or eating lunch? Or surrounded by noisy, distracting children? Or sitting in a totally darkened room—or in front of a bright open window?

There's a right way to do video chats and lots of wrong ways to do them. If you want to look good, sound good, and act good online, consider these tips and tricks for better video chats.

Creating the Right Environment

Let's start with the room where you chat. The right environment—including the lighting, the room itself, and what's in the room—makes you look good without drawing attention to itself.

Find a Quiet Place—and Close the Door

In most cases, the best place to chat is in a dedicated room without anything else going on. You want a quiet space with no background noises that might distract you or the people with whom you're chatting.

This may be difficult in your home. Maybe you don't have a dedicated office or a spare room. Maybe you're forced to video chat from your living room or bedroom or kitchen table. Maybe you're sharing your space with a spouse or kids or grandkids or roommates.

If privacy is impossible, then you just have to try to deal with it. To help you concentrate and muffle ambient noise, you can use headphones (noise-cancelling ones are best) or earbuds. You also should make judicious use of the mute button when you're not talking, so people don't have to listen to everything going on in the background when you're not talking. And you can position yourself with your back to a wall so that people won't be seen behind you.

You may, however, want more privacy than that—especially when on business or more professional calls. For this kind of video chat, you want the room empty and quiet, and you want to make sure to shut the door so other people (or animals) don't walk in on you when you're chatting. We've all seen videos of talking heads on TV news shows joining in from home and their kids walking in on them while they're live on the air. (Here's one of my favorites, from an interview on the BBC: youtu.be/Mh4f9AYRCZY.) It can happen to the best of us, but you want to try to reduce the odds of it happening to you. Go into your office or bedroom or spare room or basement, close the door, and put a note on the outside telling people not to enter when the door's closed. That should help.

Park Your Pets

I've been on calls where pets have been the center of attention, jumping up between a caller and the camera to get a little love. In some calls, they have decidedly not been welcome. In those cases, although you can't control when your dog decides to bark, you can put your pets in another room while you're chatting—and make sure the door stays closed!

Clean Up Your Room

Remember, when you're video chatting, people see not only you, but—if you're not using a virtual background—they see the room behind and a little around you. Stop and look behind you right now. Is this what you want people to see?

If not, then you need to change it. Start by picking things up. Nobody wants to see your dirty clothes on the floor, an unmade bed, or even empty bottles and coffee mugs on your desk. Take a few minutes before any video call to tidy up.

You may even want to move things around a bit. You don't have to rearrange all your furniture, but maybe you want to move some pillows or knick-knacks or that big stack of paperwork on your desk. Just clean it up a little.

Keep It Private

Speaking of paperwork, make sure there's nothing in the camera shot that's private or confidential. That could be papers from work or your most recent bank statement. If you can't move it, turn it over or put something on top of it.

A clean space gives video participants less distracting stuff to look at. If the room around you looks like a hurricane just blew through, that's not going to reflect well on you. If your room looks like a college dorm room after a Friday night party, clean it or find a different room.

Choose a Better Background

After you've cleaned up a bit, take another look behind you. What are you sitting in front of? Is it a plain wall, a group of family pictures, or a cluttered bookshelf? Are you positioned in front of a doorway to another room in your home, or an open window?

Your background reflects on you. Not only can the wrong background be distracting, but it can also paint the wrong picture of who you are.

If you want to appear professional, arrange things so that your background reflects that. Maybe you want to position yourself in front of a bookcase—but if so, make sure you have the right books in camera view. Hide the controversial stuff.

If you want to project a fun image, then put something fun behind you. If you want to show off your home, sit so that there's a full view of the living room behind you.

You definitely want to avoid a distracting background. To be honest, whenever I see someone sitting in front of a bookcase, I'm craning my neck to see what books that person is reading—instead of listening to that person talk. (I also like looking at people's kitchens, if they're really nice.) For the same reason, you probably want to remove any really distracting or controversial artwork from any wall you're sitting in front of. (Unless, that is, you want to show off your art collection.)

That said, you don't want your background to be too plain and sterile. Sitting in front of a plain white wall makes your face stand out, but it doesn't say anything about your personality. Try moving in a houseplant or something to make the space look a little more lived in.

Virtual Backgrounds

Zoom and many other video chat platforms offer virtual backgrounds within their apps, and several websites also offer virtual backgrounds anyone can use. (See Chapter 4, "Getting More Out of Zoom," for a list.) Just select the background image of your choice and the app automatically inserts it behind you.

Improve the Lighting

Dim light is the bane of many a video chatter. Let's face it; people can't see your lovely face if you're sitting in the dark.

In addition, many lower-quality cameras simply don't work well in low light. If the light's too low, you might get an overly grainy picture with muted colors.

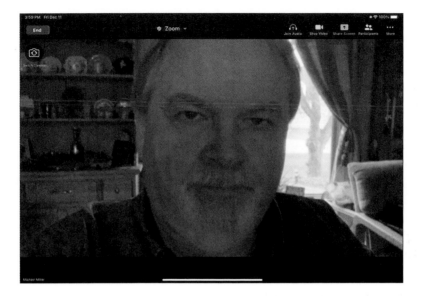

Video chatting with not enough light in front (and too much behind!)

Video chatting with better lighting

There are several things you can do to improve the lighting in your video chats. Position those lights in front of you, never behind. If it's daytime, try opening the curtains—again, as long as the window is in front or beside you, but not behind. You might also be able to put more light on your face by using a desk lamp.

It's Not All Good

Avoid Backlighting

Extra lighting is good—unless it's behind you. When you sit in front of a bright light source, such as a floor lamp or open window, the camera adjusts to that light and puts your face further into the dark. You do not want light behind you to overwhelm the light in front of you. For that reason, avoid sitting in front of a window or lamp. It's not good.

The best lighting, by the way, isn't directly in front of your face. Placing the light source at about a 45-degree angle to your face is more flattering.

If you don't have a good natural or artificial light source, invest in an external LED light. There are several designed just for video chatting and shooting YouTube videos.

External Lights

Learn more about external lighting in Chapter 13, "Enhancing Your Video Chats with Add-Ons and Accessories."

Change the Camera Position

One of my personal pet peeves is the way many people in video chats are looking down at their cameras—that is, the cameras are below eye level. This angle gives other participants a great view of chins and noses, which is less than ideal.

Video chatting with the camera sitting too low and the subject looking down

Video chatting with the camera positioned higher and the subject looking straight ahead

The problem is that most people sit their laptops or tablets on a desk or table, or hold their phones in their laps. That gives you that frumpy looking-down look, which is not flattering.

Instead of looking down at the camera—whether that's the camera in your laptop, smartphone, or tablet—you should be looking straight into the camera lens. To make this happen, you have to raise your camera—position your laptop or tablet several inches higher than the desk or table top, or hold your phone up at eye level.

One way to raise your device is to set it on a stack of books or something similar. I've written some very thick books in my time, and they work great as an impromptu tablet or laptop riser.

Another approach is to purchase a stand or tripod for your device. If you do a lot of video chatting, this is one expense that may be worth it.

Stands and Tripods

Learn more about stands and tripods in Chapter 13.

This also brings up the issue of how close to your device you should be sitting. Some people sit so close that their face fills the screen; others sit so far back that other participants see everything from the waist up.

Experts recommend that you sit far enough back so that your image takes up about 75% of the screen height. Leave a little space above your head and show the top of your shoulders, but no more. If you can't see your shoulders, you're too close; if you can see your belly, you're too far away.

>>>Go Further

CHANGE YOUR DEVICE

The device you use for video chatting makes a difference in how you appear. Some devices have better cameras than others—and the quality of the camera makes all the difference.

If you're dissatisfied with the quality of your picture in video chats, try connecting with a different device. Many laptop computers, for example, have mediocre built-in cameras. You can purchase an external webcam to replace that built-in camera, or you could simply use your phone or tablet. Most phones—and some tablets—have much better cameras than you find in the typical laptop, or even in some webcams.

Since most video chat platforms work across all different devices, it's easy to log in with your account on a different device. Try chatting with your phone, your tablet, or your computer and see which device delivers the best picture. You may be surprised!

Making a Better Connection

If you're experiencing unexpected freezes or stuttering audio or video during your video chats, you may have connection problems. You may need to improve your wireless Wi-Fi network, upgrade your Internet plan, or make other changes to ensure that your technology doesn't let you down.

Improve Your Wi-Fi Connection

Most technical issues during video chats are caused by weak Wi-Fi connections. If you're like most people, you connect to the Internet in your home via a Wi-Fi wireless network. You have a wireless router or gateway connected to an incoming Internet connection (typically through a cable modem or something similar), and that router or gateway beams the Wi-Fi signal throughout your home.

The problem, in many homes, is that the Wi-Fi signal isn't the same strength throughout. The signal is very strong close to the router, but the further away you get, the weaker the signal gets. If the Wi-Fi signal gets too weak, you don't have enough signal to carry out a seamless video chat. (Just so you know—video chatting is a fairly demanding activity, Wi-Fi and Internet bandwidth-wise.)

It's important that you test your Wi-Fi signal before you start your video chat—and from the location where you'll be chatting. The easiest way to do this is with a free service called Speedtest. You can access the service from its website (www.speedtest.net) or with the Speedtest app on your phone or tablet, which is downloadable from your device's app store. Speedtest will test the Internet signal reaching your particular device; the faster the download and upload speeds, the better.

For video chatting, you need at least 2 Mbps (that's megabits per second) both upload and download for smooth video. Obviously, anything faster than this is just gravy.

If you're not achieving these speeds, the problem could be in the Internet connection coming into your home (which I discuss in the "Upgrade Your Internet Plan" section later in this chapter), but it's more likely due to a weak Wi-Fi signal. This can be caused by too much distance between your device and your router, too many interfering structures between your device and the router, or too many other devices trying to use the Internet at the same time.

Here are a few things you can try to improve your Wi-Fi signal:

- Move your device closer to your Wi-Fi router, or vice versa. This issue is a particular problem in large homes, where the distance from one end to another is just too far for the Wi-Fi signal to reach. If you can't move your router (and most folks can't; it's stuck where it is because that's where the cable comes into your house), then move your device to increase the signal.

- Wi-Fi signals can be blocked by nearby electronic devices, metal objects, and even thick walls. If you have your router buried among other similar equipment, clear some breathing room around it. If you live in a house with very thick walls and doors, open the door to the room your router or device is in. Try repositioning the router, even if it's just a few feet, to get it away from any possible blockage or interference.

- If your home is really large or oddly shaped or has really thick walls, consider investing in a Wi-Fi extender or mesh network. Both of these technologies work similarly, in that the extender or additional mesh routers boost the Wi-Fi signal so it goes farther. You position these additional devices between your router and where your device is, so that you end up getting a stronger signal.

Call a Pro

Installing routers and extenders is much easier to do these days than it was even five or six years ago. Still, if you're uncomfortable dealing with this level of technical equipment, call an expert. Your cable company or ISP may offer installation services if you buy or rent the equipment from them. Best Buy has its Geek Squad for this kind of thing, and Office Depot and Office Max offer similar services. You also can search online for other local computer support companies that will do the job.

- If you have a dual-band router, try switching frequencies. Without getting too technical, a dual-band router broadcasts over two different wireless frequencies, 2.4 GHz and 5 GHz. (Older single-band routers only use the 2.4 GHz band.) The 2.4 GHz signal typically travels farther but can easily get overloaded with other devices connecting. The 5 GHz signal doesn't go as far, but it supports faster speeds and typically isn't as overused. Try switching the Wi-Fi network to which your device connects to the other one and see if that helps. (Again, this is fairly technical, so you may want to enlist the help of a computer support specialist.)

Switching between 2.4 GHz and 5 GHz networks on an Android phone

Connect via Ethernet Instead of Wi-Fi

Sometimes you just can't get a good enough Wi-Fi signal to support smooth video chatting. In these instances, you may be able to connect your laptop or desktop computer to your router via a wired Ethernet connection. Ethernet is both faster and more reliable than a wireless Wi-Fi signal. That makes it ideal for anything requiring large amounts of bandwidth, such as video chatting.

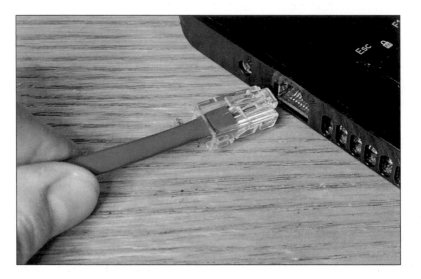

Connecting an Ethernet cable to a computer

Some newer homes are wired for Ethernet; most older homes aren't. If an Ethernet connection is nearby, or if your computer is close enough to your router that you can easily string an Ethernet cable between the two, consider doing so. Most routers and computers have Ethernet ports on the back for this purpose.

Computers Only

While there are rather arcane and complicated ways to connect phones and tablets to Ethernet, in general Ethernet is for computers only. Most laptop and desktop computers come with Ethernet connections built-in. (Apple's Mac laptops are the exception here; they require an Ethernet-to-USB adapter to connect to Ethernet.)

Minimize Network Traffic

Too many people doing too many things on the Internet can overload both your wireless Wi-Fi network and your Internet connection. There's only so much bandwidth available; if someone's trying to watch a streaming movie on the living room TV, someone else is watching YouTube videos on their phone, and yet another household resident is playing online games, you may have no bandwidth left to experience a smooth video chat.

The solution is simple—kick some of those people off the network!

Well, that sounds simpler than it might be, but it really is the solution when there's too much traffic on your home network. Maybe you need to ask someone to pause the movie until your video chat is over.

Close Unused Applications

Video chat is a demanding application and it can overload your computer or mobile device—especially if you have lots of other apps running in the background. Some of that freezing and stuttering could be caused by your device not having enough oomph to keep up with everything you're trying to do.

In this instance, the solution is truly in your hands. You need to close all the apps and windows that you're not using. Create a relatively clean environment for your video chat, and you'll experience fewer unwanted interruptions.

Upgrade Your Internet Plan

Finally, know that video chat uses a lot of Internet bandwidth. If you have a lower-priced plan from your Internet service provider (ISP), you may want to consider upgrading to a plan that offers faster speeds (which equates to more bandwidth). For that matter, you may be able to get a faster plan at a similar price from another ISP if there are competing companies in your area. (Many people don't.) If you're doing a lot of video chatting—especially if you're relying on video chat for distance learning or business meetings—paying a few extra bucks a month for faster Internet may be worth it.

How much speed is enough? It all depends on what you're doing and how many people are doing it. To be honest, if it's just you video chatting and nobody else doing much of anything else online, you can get by with a basic 10 Mbps or so plan. However, if your spouse or significant other or progeny are also video chatting at the same time, then you need to double (or triple, depending on how many people are online) that number. And if others in your home are watching YouTube or Netflix or whatever while you're trying to video chat, then you need to go for a 50 Mbps or 100 Mbps plan at the minimum.

Many households started to experience bandwidth issues during the COVID-19 crisis because adults started working from home (and doing a lot of Zoom meetings) and children were learning remotely (also with a lot of Zooming) at the same time. If you have three or four or more people video chatting simultaneously, it's easy to overload your Internet connection—especially on the upload bandwidth.

It's Not All Good

Upload Limitations

For many reasons, most Internet service providers have significantly slower upload speeds than download speeds. Traditionally, more people passively downloaded videos and other content than they uploaded files, so ISPs put more emphasis on download speeds than upload speeds.

That's changed with video chatting, as uploading is as important and as demanding as downloading. (You download others' voice and picture and upload your own, simultaneously.) So even if you have a fast Internet plan, your uploading may be constrained. In some instances, a more costly plan may include faster upload speeds, too, but that isn't always a given.

Improving Your Appearance

How you look onscreen is important. The best lighting in the world won't matter if you're wearing a ratty t-shirt or baggy pajamas while you're chatting with someone important. You need to pay attention to your appearance—and how you act onscreen.

Dress Appropriately

The bottom line first: You need to dress appropriately for the situation. Unless you're having an online slumber party or catching up with your best pal, that might mean changing out of your pajamas. If it's a casual chat, you're probably okay in sweats or a t-shirt. If it's a chat with people who aren't close friends or family, change into a nicer shirt. If it's a business meeting, dress as you would in the office—business casual, probably.

Unless you're guesting on a cable news show or doing an online job interview, you probably don't need to put on a suit and tie or formal business wear. You just need to be appropriate—no faded old t-shirts with inappropriate or controversial slogans or images.

However you dress, keep the onscreen visuals in mind. Avoid wearing tops with intricate patterns that might cause weird visual effects. That means no tight stripes or plaids. Bold and bright colors are good, as long as they don't blend into or clash with your background.

Avoid tops that might make you look topless if you sit too close to the camera. Also avoid clothing that might give viewers an inappropriate peek if your camera is positioned at the wrong angle.

It's also a good idea to avoid too much jewelry or big and jangly items. You don't want shiny jewelry catching the light and flashing in the eyes of the other participants.

Then there's the issue of pants. In most instances, you're only going to be visible from the chest up, and no one will see what you're wearing below the belt—unless, that is, you have the occasion to stand up while you're chatting, which sometimes happens. While it's likely that no one will see if you're wearing shorts or sweats with your business casual top, you don't want to risk it in case they do get a glimpse.

In other words, just be appropriate—top to bottom.

Do Your Hair and Look Presentable

You should make sure you comb or brush your hair; it's easy to forget about that when you're not venturing out in public much. You don't have to go overboard; just make sure you look presentable.

Do you need to wear makeup when you're chatting from home? All makeup is a matter of personal style and taste, but if you typically do wear makeup, you might want to wear a little. If you go the cosmetics route, do a trial run to see how you look on camera and adjust accordingly.

Use Zoom's Beauty Filter

If you're chatting with Zoom, there's a setting that could make you look better onscreen. From within a Zoom meeting, select More and then select Meeting Settings. From there, you can switch on the Touch Up My Appearance option. (On a Mac, select Video Settings, Video, then Touch Up My Appearance.) This feature supposedly softens the appearance of your skin. Your mileage will vary, of course; I noticed very little effect on my wizened old face.

Get Comfortable

When you're setting up a video chat, arrange your environment for your comfort. You may be sitting in front of that camera for a long time, and you need to be comfortable. Make sure you have a comfy chair and that it's properly adjusted—or, if you're sitting on your couch or bed, that you're in a comfortable position. It's a good idea to have water or another beverage within arm's reach if your mouth gets dry. And if you need any supporting materials during your chat, have them out and available ahead of time; you don't want to rush off camera to grab something in the middle of a call.

Minimize Distractions

Make sure, to the best of your ability, that there's little to distract you during the course of the video chat. That means closing the door (if you can), silencing your phone, and maybe even putting your phone somewhere out of reach, so you're not tempted to check your messages during the chat.

Close all the other apps and windows on your computer or device, so you won't get any distracting notifications during your video chat. Avoid rustling papers and making other distracting noises in the background. Out of courtesy, look at the screen and give participants your full attention. As much as you can, avoid multitasking while you're chatting. And, by all means, don't snack while you're chatting; that's just insulting to the other participants.

If you must do something else, even typing, consider muting your audio and turning off your camera. You don't need to let everyone else know that you're doing something else instead of paying attention.

Don't Fidget

We all know that some video chats get boring and go on too long. Just don't let your boredom be apparent.

That means sitting *still* for the course of the chat. Don't rock back and forth, don't spin your chair, and don't wheel it around the room. Don't look out the window or get up to wander around the room. Even messing with your hair can be distracting. If you must fidget, do it quietly and offscreen.

Look at the Camera—Not Yourself

When you're video chatting, locate your device's camera and look directly at it. (Your device might have a small light indicating when the camera is active; that's where you should look.) It's tempting to look at your thumbnail onscreen. Don't. (Some platforms have a function of hiding your self-view, which can help you focus on the camera.) Even though it's just inches onscreen from your thumbnail to your device's camera, it's obvious to others when you're not looking at the camera. It looks as if you're not paying attention.

This also means that, at least when you're talking, you shouldn't look at other people in the chat. A person's face onscreen is not where the camera is. It may be difficult at first, but don't look at the screen—look at the camera.

Mute Yourself—and Remember to Unmute

When you're chatting with more than one other person, especially in larger video meetings, you don't want to subject everybody else to any distracting background noises. When you're not talking, mute your microphone. Just remember to unmute your mic when it's your turn to talk again—there's little more embarrassing than someone's lips moving and no sound coming out. "You're muted" and "unmute yourself" might be the most frequent expressions in the video chat lexicon.

Know Your Audience

When you're judging your appearance in a video chat, you want to be pretty much on the same level as all the other participants. If everybody else is dressed business casual, you don't want to be wearing a dirty sweatshirt. On the other hand, if everybody is wearing t-shirts or sweaters, you don't want to be the only one in a suit and tie.

The same goes with your environment. If most people are chatting from their living rooms, you don't need to be in a professional video studio with fancy lights and a clever background. Vice versa, of course; if everybody else is chatting from their home offices, sitting in your bedroom with the open bathroom door behind you probably won't cut it.

However you're chatting, you want to be as good as everybody else—but not a lot better. You want to fit in with the group, as much as possible.

Test Before You Chat

To check your appearance and background onscreen and to make sure your camera and microphone are properly selected and working, you should test your audio and video before you chat. Many video chat platforms include an option for previewing your video and audio before a call starts. With other platforms, you can launch a new call without any other participants to see how you look. That gives you the opportunity to make any necessary corrections before the real chat starts.

Preparing for a Video Meeting

To make your video chats more efficient, you need to prepare for them ahead of time. Now, if you're just having a quick chat with a sibling or grandkid, you don't have to do a lot prep work. But if you have a business or small group meeting coming up, it pays to do your homework ahead of time.

Tips If You're Hosting a Video Meeting

If you're hosting a video meeting with more than one other participant, you don't want to waste their time. Here are some tips on how you can run a more efficient video meeting:

- Check all your equipment, as well as your Internet connection, ahead of the chat, to avoid getting sidelined by technical issues.

- Start on time.

- When the chat starts, let people know if you are recording the video chat.

If you're hosting a more official meeting, follow these tips:

- Make it clear to all participants what the rules of the meeting are—whether they need to take notes, whether you've enabled text chat, whether they're expected to participate or just watch, that sort of thing.

- Email participants an agenda and any materials they might need to help them prepare.

- Once the chat gets going, stick to a schedule; don't let side discussions derail the meeting and make sure you end at the promised time.

- A few minutes before the end of the meeting, wrap things up and summarize what you've accomplished.

Finally, when it's time to sign off, make sure you thank everyone for their time. And, if you've recorded the meeting, you can send everyone the link to the recorded file after the meeting ends.

Tips If You're Participating in a Formal Video Meeting

When you're participating in a more formal video meeting, here are some tips you keep in mind about planning for that chat:

- Review any materials sent to you in advance.

- Make sure you're familiar with the agenda and what's expected of you.

- Be on time.

- Pay attention and be prepared in case you're called on to make a comment or answer a question.

- When you do have an opportunity to speak, and it's a larger meeting with a lot of people you don't know, identify yourself when it's your turn at bat.

- If you have something to say to a particular individual, use the meeting's text chat function; don't have personal conversations in a group meeting.

- Don't multitask during the meeting; you can do your other work later.

- Stay through the entire meeting unless you have a very good reason to cut out early.

Be Understanding

Whether you're a host or a participant, it's important to give a little grace to the other attendees. Not everybody is a pro at this video meeting thing; not everybody knows all the rules and etiquette. It's also not easy to pick up on social cues when chatting online, so there might be some talking out of order or talking over one another. Don't get stressed about it. We're all human and we're all (well, at least most of us) trying our best.

>>>Go Further
TIPS FOR VIDEO CHATTING WITH CHILDREN

Video chatting with the younger members of your family requires a special skill. The younger the child, the more challenging it will be for that child to stay engaged for the entire length of a video call.

When you want to stay in touch with your grandchildren or other young relatives, you need to involve them in the conversation just as if they were in the room with you. These long-distance video chats are as important to them as they are to you; you just have to learn how to make the most of them.

The first thing to do is to chat during the right time of day. Don't chat too late or they'll be too tired to concentrate. Also avoid chatting around meal time or snack time (too hungry) or at other times that might interrupt their normal routine.

Try to engage the youngsters by asking questions—simple ones they can easily answer. You can play games, read (short) stories, sing songs, even move around the room with your phone or tablet to give them a virtual tour. Do things that are interesting for them. My grandkids like to look at our dog while we're chatting—and the dog sometimes likes it, too.

You can also use screensharing to tell stories to the kiddos. Open up an ebook in one window and then share it onscreen while you read.

One last thing. Video chats don't have to be lengthy—and with kids, probably shouldn't be. Young children will lose interest long before you do, and that's okay. Multiple quick chats are better than infrequent longer ones—and always remember to tell the kids you love them.

In this chapter, you learn about various pieces of gear you can use to create a better video chat experience.

→ Webcams and Microphones
→ Headphones, Headsets, and Earbuds
→ Lighting and Backgrounds
→ Stands and Tripods

Enhancing Your Video Chats with Add-Ons and Accessories

Have you ever noticed someone in a video chat who just looks better and sounds better than the other participants—especially you? Well, you can follow all the tips and tricks I laid out in the previous chapter and still not look or sound great onscreen. Although the average video chatter might not truly need any of this equipment, there is some optional gear that could go a long way toward making a better looking and sounding video chat.

Webcams and Microphones

The pieces of equipment that are most important are those that literally put your picture onscreen and your voice through everyone's speakers: the camera and microphone.

Webcams

If you're video chatting via a phone or tablet, just skip this section. But if you video chat on your computer, the quality of your camera makes a big difference.

First, if you have a desktop or all-in-one computer, it probably doesn't include a camera or microphone. If your computer doesn't have a built-in camera or microphone, if you want to video chat, you need to buy an external webcam, which includes a camera and microphone all in one compact device.

If you have a laptop computer, it's a different deal. Almost all laptops come with a built-in camera and microphone, although the quality of these built-in cameras is often lacking. In particular, many laptop cameras are low resolution and don't perform great in low-light situations. While you can use your laptop's built-in camera, you'll probably get better results from a higher-quality (and higher-resolution) external webcam.

Logitech C920S HD webcam

Almost all webcams clip on or sit on top of your computer monitor. Webcams connect to your desktop or laptop computer with a USB cable. It's usually a simple setup—just connect the webcam's USB cable to a USB port on your computer. In most instances, your computer automatically recognizes the webcam and starts using it; in some instances, you may need to go through a separate setup routine or install a software program to configure the webcam.

When you connect a webcam to a laptop computer that already has a built-in camera, you'll probably have to manually select which camera and microphone you want to use when you log into your video chat program. Most platforms display a list of available devices, and all you have to do is pick yours from the list. (If your webcam is the only such device installed, it's probably selected by default.)

Bad Picture

If the picture from your laptop camera or webcam looks grainy, especially when the lights are low, it's a light issue. If the picture looks blocky, particularly on larger screens, it's a resolution issue.

>>>Go Further
RESOLUTION

Resolution tells you how sharp an image is. It's measured in pixels, which are the small "picture elements" that make up the onscreen images. The higher the resolution—the number of pixels in a given area—the sharper the picture.

Many older laptops and webcams had very low resolution, typically in the 640 × 480 pixel range. Modern laptops typically go a little better than that; 1280 × 720 pixel resolution (called simply 720p) is the minimum acceptable resolution today.

Many webcams and laptop cameras offer true high-definition picture quality, with a resolution of 1920 × 1080 pixels (called 1080p). Some webcams have even higher resolution, with so-called 4K or Ultra High Definition (UHD) 3840 × 2160 pixel resolution.

Note that resolution also plays a big role in the quality of picture generated by the cameras in smartphones and tablets. Most phones and tablets have cameras that are capable of 1080p video in their rear cameras, although front cameras sometimes offer lower 720p resolution.

The quality and type of lens used in the camera also affect the picture quality. Some webcams offer additional features, such as autofocus, automatic brightness, and automatic color correction, that can result in a better picture.

There are lots of good webcams out there, from companies such as Aluratek, Logitech, NexiGo, and Razer. If you're looking for high resolution, you should probably stay away from the very lowest-priced (less than $25) models because they won't have the best lenses or picture-enhancing features. Instead, set your sights on something a little more expensive (but still less than $100), such as the Logitech C920S HD (www.logitech.com), which offers features such as 1080p resolution, wide-angle lens, autofocus, and automatic light correction.

Higher-priced webcams also offer features such as 4K resolution, stereo microphones, and built-in LED lights. Look for those features you think you'll use; you probably don't need all the features of the highest-priced models.

It's Not All Good

Webcam Privacy

You need a webcam or built-in video camera to participate in video chats, but you don't want that camera spying on you when you're not using it. Unfortunately, there have been instances of malware that can infect your computer, hijack your camera or webcam, and use that camera to spy on you when you're not aware. It's rare, but it has happened.

To better protect your privacy, look for a webcam that offers some sort of privacy shutter. This is typically a plastic flap you can close to cover the camera lens when the camera is not in use. It's just an added form of physical protection.

Microphones

If you're video chatting on your computer, an external microphone is another accessory to consider. Often, the microphone built into your laptop or webcam is functional at best. If you want really clear, distinct sound for your voice, look into a high-quality external microphone.

Blue Snowball iCE USB microphone

A good microphone does more than just capture the sound of your voice. A quality microphone makes your voice clearer, cuts out background noise, and maybe even shapes the characteristics of your voice to give it more depth and tone. You'll never sound like a radio DJ with your computer or webcam mic; you might with the right external microphone.

The Right Equipment Makes All the Difference

I do a lot of guest spots and interviews with radio shows and podcasts across the country, and I almost always get compliments on the sound of my voice—but it's not because I naturally sound like a late-night DJ. It's because I use a professional-quality microphone, along with other pro gear. My voice sounds good because I use the right equipment. The right gear truly does matter.

When you're choosing an external microphone, choose one that connects to your computer with a USB cable. (Not all mics do; many professional-quality mics connect to pro audio equipment via what is called an XLR connector.) You can spend anywhere from $25 to more than $200 on a quality USB microphone, although you don't have to spend hundreds of dollars to make a big difference in your sound.

For example, the Blue Snowball iCE (www.bluemic.com) is one of the more popular mics for video chatting and recording podcasts and YouTube video commentaries. It sells for around $50 and plugs directly into any USB port on your computer. Other popular USB mics are available from Apogee, ATR, Blue, JLAB Audio, Shure, and similar companies.

Headset Mics

You can also go with a headset that includes both headphones and a small microphone, as discussed in the next section. The mics included in these headsets are okay for casual video chats but not as good as the USB mics you can buy separately.

When you're using an external microphone, you need to check the settings of your video chat app. Look for the audio or audio/video section and make sure that your external microphone (not your device's internal mic) is selected.

Microphone Tips

When you're using an external microphone, get close to it but not too close. Place your microphone 6 inches or so from your mouth, and make sure it's directly in front of your mouth, not above, below, or to the side.

>>>Go Further

USING A USB MICROPHONE WITH YOUR PHONE OR TABLET

Your phone or tablet doesn't have a USB connector, so how do you use a USB microphone, like the Blue Snowball iCE, with your mobile device? The answer is simple—just connect the mic's USB plug to a USB-to-Lightning (for most iPhones and iPads) or a USB to USB-C (for Android phones and some newer iOS devices) adapter, depending on which type of connector your device has, and then connect the other end to your phone or tablet. Your device should recognize the microphone and switch to that input for all chatting and recording.

Headphones, Headsets, and Earbuds

Making sure that all your chat buddies can see and hear you clearly is important. It's equally important that you can hear them well. You can increase the quality of incoming sound by replacing your normal speaker with a set of quality headphones or earbuds.

Using headphones or earbuds in place of your device's built-in speaker also eliminates the echo you sometimes hear when your device's microphone picks up other people talking in your chat. With your speaker off, there's nothing extraneous for your microphone to pick up.

Which Is Which?

Some definitions are in order. *Headphones* cover your ears with large earpads and are for listening only. A *headset* is essentially headphones with a microphone attached. *Earbuds* are small devices that fit into your ears, not over them. Many earbuds have a microphone built into the cable.

Headphones

One problem some people have with video chatting is dealing with all the other noises in their house. Dogs barking, kids yelling, television playing, neighbors cutting the grass—all these background noises can be real distractions.

One way to minimize the background noise is to use a set of quality head-phones instead of the speaker inside your computer or mobile device. The headphones' earpads sit on top of or cover your ears, thus blocking out a lot of that extraneous noise. (They're also good for listening to music.)

Sony WH-XB900N wireless noise-cancelling headphones

Even better, invest in a set of noise-cancelling headphones. So-called *passive* noise-cancelling phones are constructed of special sound-absorbing materials that block specific frequencies. More expensive *active* noise-cancelling phones employ special circuitry to identify and block low-frequency sounds before they reach your ears.

Some headphones are wireless, connecting to your device via Bluetooth, whereas most are wired and connect via your device's auxiliary headphone jack. You can spend as little as $10 or as much as $500 for a set of phones, from companies like Audio-Technica, Bose, JBL, Sennheiser, and Sony. For example, the Sony WH-XB900N (www.sony.com/electronics/headband-headphones/wh-xb900n) offers Bluetooth wireless connectivity and active noise-cancelling technology and typically sells for less than $150. Obviously, the more you spend, the better the sound—and, most often, the more comfortable the fit.

Headsets

A headset is essentially a set of headphones with a built-in microphone. The microphone typically attaches to one of the earpads and swivels in front of your mouth.

A headset replaces your device's built-in speakers and microphone, eliminating the need for a separate external mic. Headsets can be either wired (typically via USB) or wireless. Some more expensive ones offer noise-cancelling technology.

Mpow Hc6 USB Headset with Microphone

Expect to pay anywhere from $30 to $300 for a quality headset, such as the Mpow Hc6 USB Headset (www.xmpow.com/products/mpow-hc6-usb-headset-with-microphone), which sells for less than $40. Other headsets are available from Jabra, Logitech, Mpow, Plantronics, and other companies.

Earbuds

If you don't like how headphones look or feel on your ears, then consider using a simple set of earbuds instead. Make sure you get earbuds with a built-in microphone and you're good to go for all your video chatting.

The earbuds that came with your phone might do the job, or you might want to invest in a set of higher-quality buds for your video chatting. Many people like to use wireless earbuds, such as Apple's AirPods (www.apple.com/airpods/); they're great if you like to walk around during or between video chats, and you don't have to worry about hiding the cable so it won't be seen on camera.

Apple's AirPods wireless earbuds

You can find regular wired earbuds for a few bucks (or more) at your local drug-store or big box retailer. Wireless earbuds start at around $30 and go up from there. (Apple's AirPods cost a little under $150.)

Lighting and Backgrounds

How you look onscreen during a video chat is important, especially during business meetings. The two most important things you can do to improve your onscreen looks (after investing in a quality webcam, of course) is to improve your lighting and what's behind you when you're on camera.

Lighting

No doubt you've been in many a video chat where your fellow participants look dark and grainy, like they're hiding in the shadows. These kinds of problems are caused by shooting without enough light on the subject. Some cameras can compensate for low lighting, to a degree, but all subjects will benefit from being shot with adequate lighting on their faces.

Let's face it, if you're sitting in shadows or darkness, the other chat participants will have trouble seeing you. If you're brightly and flatteringly lit, on the other hand, you look much more appealing; people will be able to see your smiling face.

Fortunately, the lighting issue is probably the cheapest and easiest one to fix. You can start (as I address in Chapter 12, "Tips and Tricks for Better Video Chats") by opening the blinds and letting in some natural light. You can turn on all the lights in your room and position them so they're in front of you rather than behind you. You can even turn on a desk lamp and shine it toward your face.

The more professional solution, however, is to invest in an external LED light kit. Some of these lights clip onto the top of your laptop or computer monitor; some come with desktop tripods; and some even include a holder for a smartphone in addition to the external light.

There are two primary types of external lights used for video chatting: LED light panels and ring lights. A light panel is literally a small panel of LEDs, no bigger than a smartphone. A ring light is a circle of LED lights, in the middle of which can fit a smartphone.

LED light panels typically put out the most light, and often can be adjusted to put out light that is warmer (more orange or red) or cooler (more blue) in color. (This is called *color temperature*; warmer lighting can give your skin a healthy glow, whereas cooler lighting can look a little more clean and energetic.) These lights typically run between $50 and $100. For example, the Lume Cube Panel Mini (www.lumecube.com/products/panel-mini) sells for $60 and offers adjustable brightness and color temperature, along with a frosted lens to diffuse the lighting.

Lume Cube Panel Mini LED light panel

Diffused Is Better Than Direct

Shining a bright light directly at your face may result in bright spots and harsh shadows. (It may also cause you to squint, which is not a good look.) A better approach is to use some sort of diffuser to soften and scatter the light before it hits your face.

Ring lights are a little less expensive, depending on the setup. Some come on short tripods, others on taller tripods, still others with holders that can hold a smartphone (or, with larger models, a tablet). As with block lights, some ring lights offer adjustable color temperature and brightness. Expect to pay anywhere from $20 to $100, depending on size and features.

AIXPI 10-inch LED ring light with tripod stand and phone holder

For example, AIXPI (www.aixpi.com/ringlights) offers ring lights in sizes from 6-inch to 18-inch diameter, with a variety of different stands and mounts. The 10-inch model with an adjustable tripod and smartphone holder runs about $25.

Professional Lighting Kits

Another option is a lighting kit like those used by professional photographers. These kits typically include two or more external lights, stands, diffusers, and more but are probably overkill for the typical video chat session.

Green Screens and Other Backgrounds

Next, think about what's behind you when you're video chatting. Maybe you set yourself up in front of a blank wall. Maybe you're in a busy room with a lot of clutter behind you. Maybe all you have is a small desk in your bedroom and your chat friends are forced to look at your unmade bed and dirty clothes.

Especially for work meetings, it's far, far better to present a cleaner and more professional background. This is why some video chat platforms, such as Zoom and Google Meet, let you add virtual backgrounds, so you can appear to be chatting from anywhere.

The problem is that you need a clean and ideally green physical background behind you for the virtual background technology to work properly. TV shows and movies use this kind of "green screen" technology all the time, where everything of a certain color in the shot is removed and replaced with another image. The most-used background is a certain shade of bright green not found in nature; remove the green and replace it with a virtual background and you're good to go.

Assuming you don't have a solid bright green wall behind you in your home, how can you achieve this type of green screen effect? The solution is to simply set up a green screen behind you. Several companies sell green muslin or paper background rolls, which are great if you have the space and time to set up.

Interfit's Studio Essentials Pop-Up Reversible Background Kit

A more convenient solution is to use a pop-up green screen, such as Interfit's Studio Essentials Pop-Up Reversible Background Kit (www.interfitphoto.com). This kit includes a 5-foot by 6.5-foot foldable double-sided green/blue background and 7.5-foot tall stand. It only takes a minute to set up the stand and unfold the background; then you're good to go with any virtual background your video chat platform provides. (The kit sells for $60.)

If you'd rather have a neutral physical background behind you, companies such as Interfit, Kate, and Studio Essentials make pop-up kits with a variety of different backgrounds.

>>>*Go Further*

WHERE TO BUY

As the Joker asked of Batman in the 1989 movie, where do you get all those wonderful toys?

Most of the items discussed in this chapter are available at various online retailers. You can find webcams, microphones, headphones, and other electronics at Amazon (www.amazon.com), Best Buy (www.bestbuy.com), Newegg (www.newegg.com), and similar retailers.

Some of the items you might need are actually carryovers from the world of professional photography—tripods, backgrounds, lighting kits, and the like. For these items, check out your local photography stores or go to Adorama (www.adorama.com) or B&H Photo (www.bhphotovideo.com) online.

Stands and Tripods

One of the things that annoys me about video chats is that so many people put their computer or phone or tablet on a table or desk and then look down at it. This results in a camera angle that goes right up the person's nose, which isn't very flattering.

The problem, of course, is how to hold your device so that the camera is at eye level. The solution is some sort of stand or tripod that raises your computer, phone, or tablet accordingly.

Laptop Stands

If you're chatting on a laptop computer, the camera is typically right above the display. Depending on the height of your desk or table, that might be close enough to eye level to work. If your desk or table is too low, however, or if you have a laptop with a smaller screen, you'll still be looking down at the camera during video chats.

The other issue is the angle of the screen. Tilting the display back to better view the screen contents may put the camera tilting upward, too, which gives you a chin-forward look. You actually want to have the top of your screen slightly above your eye level facing straight forward, which is tough to achieve on its own.

Although you could attempt to solve this problem by setting your laptop on top of several really thick books, you can also invest in a stand that lifts the entire device several inches and puts the screen and camera at the best angle for your video calls.

Rain Design's mStand laptop stand

Buying a stand for your laptop is a great way to get a better angle while you are on calls. There are lots of different laptop stands out there in all sorts of designs and configurations, so choose one that best fits your needs and the physical dimensions of your laptop. You probably want something simple like the Rain Design mStand (www.raindesigninc.com/mstand.html), which sells for about $45. Other laptop stands are available from other companies, typically in the $20 to $60 range.

External Keyboards

If your laptop sits on a stand, you may find the keyboard difficult to use. An external keyboard of some sort may be a good investment; consider a wireless one for the most convenient setup.

Tablet Stands

You run into the same height issue when using an iPad or other tablet for video chatting. You need a stand that lifts your tablet up to eye level and holds it steady while you're chatting.

There are a ton of different tablet stands out there, some specific to Apple's iPad, but most that work with all brands of tablets. Make sure you get one for your tablet's specific dimensions; a stand designed for an iPad mini will probably not work with a larger iPad Pro.

AboveTEK's Flexible Arm Stand for tablets

The taller tablet stands that you need typically run anywhere from $15 to $60. For example, the AboveTEK Flexible Arm Stand (www.abovetek.com) fits most tablets and can raise your iPad up to 1.3 feet above desk level. It's at the high end of prices for stands, selling for about $60.

Typing Stands

If you're on a budget, consider placing your tablet on a simple typing stand, the kind used to hold papers and other documents when you're typing. These typically run around $10 and are available from most any office supply store. (If you do a lot of typing, you may already have one of these around the house!)

Tripods

If you're video chatting on your phone, holding your phone for an entire video call can become tiresome. You may be able to lean it against something on your desk, but you may want to invest in a tripod for your phone. There are lots of different models available, priced anywhere from $15 to $50. For example, the UBeesize Phone Tripod (www.ubeesize.com) extends from a minimum height of 20 inches all the way to 51 inches if you want to stand it on the floor. It sells for about $22. Similar tripods are available from Aureday, Fugetek, Joby, and other companies.

UBeesize Phone Tripod

You can also find tripods and stands for webcams. A tripod lets you position the webcam wherever you want it, even off to the side of your computer or monitor.

Most webcams fit on phone or camera tripods. You can also find dedicated webcam stands, like the InnoGear Webcam Stand (www.innogear.com), which uses a flexible gooseneck that lets you position your webcam just about any way you want. It costs less than $20. Similar webcam stands are available from Amada, Pipshell, Sigsit, and other companies.

InnoGear Webcam Stand

>>>Go Further

ADD-ON APPS TO ENHANCE ZOOM MEETINGS

If you're a frequent Zoom user, know that there is a Zoom App Marketplace full of add-on apps to enhance your Zoom meetings. (Access the Zoom App Marketplace at marketplace.zoom.us/.) Most of these apps are targeted at business users, and most come with monthly subscription fees, often on a per-user basis.

What types of apps can you find in the Zoom App Marketplace? Some of my favorites include Appointlet, which lets counselors and business people schedule appointments from within Zoom; Lingmo Translate, which translates Zoom text chats into different languages in real time; and SurveyMonkey, which lets you create real-time surveys for your Zoom meetings and seminars. There are also Zoom apps that let you connect Zoom to other productivity apps, including Evernote, Google's G Suite, Microsoft Teams, Salesforce, and Slack.

14

Hosting Virtual Events

Platforms like FaceTime, Facebook Messenger, and Zoom are great for one-on-one or small group chats, but you can also use video chat to host larger events. When family, friends, and colleagues can't gather in person, a remote meeting or celebration is a great alternative, with everybody in the comfort of their own homes. There are also events where participants are more passive, such as online conferences, seminars, and webinars. Hosting a larger gathering of either type is really just an extension of the smaller chats you already know how to do.

What Is a Virtual Event?

A *virtual event* is any organized event held via a video chat platform. These events can range from small family get-togethers where everyone participates to large business conferences where there are speakers and passive attendees.

Types of Virtual Events

When you host a virtual event of any type, you invite your participants, normally with advance notice, and they join you in a large chat room. Some events encourage participation from everyone attending; others are presentations where the attendees just sit and watch.

Personal events can include

- Anniversary parties
- B'nai mitzvahs
- Birthday parties
- Family gatherings
- Game nights
- Graduation parties
- Holiday celebrations
- Movie-watching parties
- Wedding receptions (and weddings!)

More organized or professional events can include any of the following—many of which went virtual when the pandemic sent us into quarantine:

- Behind-the-scenes tours
- Classes
- Concerts
- Conferences
- Question-and-answer sessions
- Seminars (webinars)
- Training courses
- Workshops

Choosing the Right Chat Platform

When you're thinking of hosting a virtual event, either personal or professional, the first thing you need to do is decide which chat platform to use. You want a platform that accommodates the number of people and the duration of meeting you want, works across all types of devices (phones, tablets, and computers), and is cross-platform (Android and Apple's iOS).

This rules out FaceTime because not all your attendees will have iPhones, iPads, and Macs. It also rules out Facebook Messenger because not all your attendees will be on Facebook. You also shouldn't choose WhatsApp, because some of your attendees will be logging on from their computers—and WhatsApp only does video chat on mobile devices. And if you're having more than 32 participants, Google Duo won't work, even though it is cross-platform.

Taking all these variables into account, you're left with those chat platforms that also cater to a business audience:

- Facebook Messenger Rooms (cross-platform, 50 attendees max)
- Google Meet (cross-platform, 100 attendees max)
- Microsoft Teams (cross-platform, 250 attendees max)
- Skype (cross-platform, 100 attendees max)
- Zoom (cross-platform, 100 attendees max)

All these platforms require the host to have an account with the service (free). Attendees do not have to have an account to attend an event; all they have to do is click a link in the invitation and then join from their web browsers.

Of these platforms, Zoom is far and away the most popular choice for both personal and professional events. Although Google Meet, Microsoft Teams, and Skype can easily handle a large number of attendees, Zoom has a slightly easier-to-use interface and a well-developed set of meeting tools. It's also the platform most people are most familiar with.

Hosting a Virtual Gathering

When you have something to celebrate or talk about but can't get everyone together in the same room, then it's time to consider hosting a virtual gathering. You can use video chat to host virtual holiday gatherings, baby showers, neighborhood parties, and more.

Plan a Virtual Event

The precise steps to launch a large video chat event differ from platform to platform, but are similar to the instructions listed previously in this book for smaller video chats. The general instructions for planning a larger virtual event, however, are the same from platform to platform. Follow these eight easy steps to get your virtual celebration up and running.

(1) **Set a date and time.** Keep your attendees' schedules in mind. If many of your attendees work during the day, don't schedule an event in the middle of the afternoon. Evenings and weekends are probably best for most personal events. You may even want to query important attendees in advance to see what days and times work best for them.

(2) **Set the length of your event.** How long would a normal celebration of this type last? Try for a little shorter than that, as people's attention can flag when they're chatting online for long periods. If you go more than an hour, schedule a break at about the one-hour mark. (And if you go three hours, schedule another break at the two-hour mark.) You don't want to impinge on the kindness of your guests for an entire afternoon or evening; when it comes to online gatherings, shorter is better than longer.

Zoom Limits

Free Zoom accounts are limited to 40-minute meetings. If you have a longer event, you have to schedule it as a series of consecutive meetings.

(3) **Assemble your guest list.** First, determine how many people you want to invite. Is it more than 10? Less than 50? A hundred or more? The number of guests helps determine which video chat platform you choose. You also want to make sure you have email addresses for everyone you want to invite.

No Shows

For any given event, about a third of the people you invite are likely to be no-shows—which means you can probably invite more people than you expect to show up.

(4) **Select the right video chat platform.** You need a platform that works on all devices and operating systems and is easy to use. Since you're probably dealing with at least some nontechnical attendees who aren't that familiar with video chat, consider Facebook Messenger Rooms (for events with 50 or fewer attendees), Skype, or Zoom.

Houseparty

If you like to play games with a small circle of friends, there's a video chat app named Houseparty you might want to check out. Houseparty runs on Android and iOS phones, lets you chat with up to eight people in a group, and includes several built-in games designed for online play. Get more details at www.houseparty.com.

(5) **Schedule the event and send the invitations.** Open your video chat platform and schedule the event. Then, while you're still in the chat program, send email invitations to everyone on your guest list. Include all the necessary information about the event, including what it's about, who it's for (if it's that kind of celebration), any theme, and the date and time. Make sure the invitation includes a web link to the online event. (Most chat platforms include that link automatically when you send invitations to attendees.) You should send out invitations at least a week prior to the event. And, if your chat platform offers the option, send out the invitation as a calendar invitation, which invitees can then save directly to their online or app-based calendars.

Include Instructions

Not everyone attending your virtual event will be equally familiar with the technology. Some may have never video chatted before. Make sure you include detailed step-by-step instructions on how to access your event, log in, use various functions (such as muting the mic and turning off the camera), and what to expect from the session. Don't leave out any details; assume your attendees know nothing and need a lot of help.

(6) **Remind attendees ahead of the event.** Ideally everyone will schedule and remember your event. That said, it's a good idea to remind people ahead of time. The day before the event, send out an email reminder to all invitees.

(7) **Test the platform and equipment.** Make sure everything works before everyone logs in. Check your computer, camera, and microphone, and make sure you have a strong Internet connection. If the chat platform allows you to log in to the room in advance, do so to make sure everything is as you want.

(8) **Launch the event.** Open your chat room and wait for everyone to arrive. If you've enabled a waiting room, grant admission to attendees as they enter. Make sure you greet everyone as they arrive!

>>>Go Further
TIPS FOR A SMOOTHER AND SAFER EVENT

Unless you're hosting an event open to the entire public, you probably want to take some steps to keep out uninvited guests—and help your event run more smoothly.

One of the best ways to keep uninvited guests out is to activate the waiting room option in your video chat platform (if it has one; Microsoft Teams and Zoom do). This way, you have control over who enters your chat. You should also require a password for entry.

Finally, to keep things from getting too chaotic, remember that you have the ability to mute and unmute people. You may want to mute everyone's audio when they first enter and then unmute them later. Remember, though, that muting everyone cuts down on the social interaction, so use this judiciously.

Manage a Virtual Celebration

Hosting an online celebration requires some specific thought. Treat your virtual celebration the same as you would a physical one. Here are some tips for managing a virtual celebration:

- **Choose a theme.** You don't want to host just another boring Zoom call; you want your event to be fun and memorable. The theme you choose can inform the invitations you send, the background you choose for yourself, and the activities you plan.

- **Plan your activities.** Depending on the type of celebration you're hosting, you may want to schedule some group games, music, maybe even a (virtual) guest visit from a magician or other performer. Trivia games, charades, karaoke, Pictionary, and scavenger hunts are good and easy to do via video chat. These activities help to break the ice and get everyone involved, so have a few up your sleeve. You don't have to plan things down to the second, but you should have a rough schedule of what you want to do and when.

- **Decorate your room—or choose a virtual background.** If your party has a theme, then decorate your room—or at least the space visible on camera—accordingly. That might just mean throwing up a banner and some balloons on the wall behind you, but the effort will be appreciated. Alternatively, find a virtual background that matches your theme and activate that.

- **Dress for the occasion.** Dress for your party—at least from the waist up. If it's a costume, themed, or dressy event, inform your guests of that fact so they can dress accordingly, too.

Icebreakers

Whatever activities you do or don't do, you might want to prepare some icebreakers to get the party started. You can go around the virtual room and ask everyone to introduce themselves or answer some sort of "get to know you" question—anything to get things moving.

- **Play some tunes.** You may want to play some background music at your virtual party. (Or maybe it's foreground music, for music trivia or karaoke.) The easiest way to do this is via screen sharing, with your favorite online music service in a window that you're sharing. Everyone will be able to hear the music as well as people talking.

- **Plan for opening gifts.** If you're hosting a party where gifts are involved, make sure to leave time to open them. Invite your guests to send their gifts in advance to the guest of honor, who can open them on camera at the designated time. (And if it's a birthday party, don't forget to sing "Happy Birthday!")

- **Keep everyone involved.** As the virtual celebration progresses, make an effort to keep everyone involved to one degree or another. You don't want anyone feeling left out and fading into the (virtual) background. That probably means making an effort to ask people questions or opinions or just to participate a little.

- **Give 'em a break.** If your party lasts longer than an hour, take a five- or ten-minute break halfway through. If it lasts more than two hours, take two breaks. If it lasts more than three hours, it's probably too long.

- **End graciously.** When the party's over, say so and thank everyone for coming. Guests always appreciate a gracious host, even if the gathering is virtual.

Whatever type of virtual celebration you host, make sure you and all your guests have fun. Even if things go wrong or your equipment acts up, roll with it and remember that your guests are there to celebrate with you. If it's not fun, you're not doing it right.

>>>Go Further
HOW TO AVOID AWKWARDNESS

Video chats and events can quickly get awkward when there are too many people in the room—or nobody knows when to talk.

This awkwardness comes in part because, in a video chat, people don't get the essential body-language cues that are part of a physical meeting. A large part of communication is nonverbal, and when you can see the other guests only from the shoulders up in a tiny window on your phone or computer screen, you just don't get those physical cues. You may not be able to tell when someone wants to speak, or they're bored, or whatever.

In addition, some people are simply reticent to step up and speak when it isn't clear it's their turn—and in a virtual gathering, it's seldom clear who speaks next unless the host prompts people. That leaves it up to you, as the host, to keep the conversation moving. You can do some advance prep by specifying an order for people to talk, or you can prompt individual guests to speak as the conversation progresses.

The goal is to create a lively conversation without leaving anyone out. Using icebreakers to get everybody comfortable is a good first step, but you may need to be more proactive throughout the entire conversation to keep things moving. Don't let awkwardness take over your virtual gatherings—make everyone feel comfortable and free to jump in.

Hosting a Webinar

The rules for hosting a meeting where participants are passive and largely muted—often called a webinar, conference, or seminar—are similar to those for more personal virtual events. It's all about choosing the right forum, putting on a good program, and being able to manage large numbers of attendees.

Choose One: Meeting or Webinar?

When it comes to choosing the right video chat platform for large virtual events, Zoom is the choice of business users worldwide. Other platforms, such as Google Meet and Microsoft Teams, are doing their best to compete with Zoom, but Zoom has a large base of users and a bevy of features designed specifically for large business meetings.

Most of these features are available only with the paid business versions of Zoom. If you work for a business that has a Zoom subscription, you'll find lots of options that aren't covered elsewhere in this book, where we focus on the free consumer version.

Free Zoom

Learn more about the free consumer version of Zoom in Chapter 3, "Using Zoom."

One of the first choices you need to make is whether you want to launch a Zoom meeting or a Zoom webinar. A Zoom meeting is like the ones you're probably familiar with from Zoom's free version—just with more people in it. A Zoom business meeting can have anywhere from 300 to 500 attendees, depending on the plan you're paying for, and they're completely interactive. That means the hosts can talk to the attendees, and the attendees can speak back (if they're not muted). Zoom business meetings also let you share the hosting duties with one or more cohosts and break the larger meeting into smaller breakout rooms.

A Zoom webinar can handle even more attendees—up to 50,000 at one time. Webinars are more presentation-oriented than interactive; attendees sit and watch what you're presenting and don't expect to speak up at all.

Which should you choose—a Zoom meeting or a webinar? It really comes down to how much interaction you want. If you want or need a lot of back and forth with and between attendees, then a Zoom business meeting is the way to go. If, on the other hand, you just want to give a presentation and don't want or need any audience feedback, a Zoom webinar is the best choice.

Hosting Tips for Webinars

Whether you're hosting a large business meeting or webinar, here are some tips to help you run a more efficient and effective large virtual event.

- **Use the right equipment.** Although you can run a large event from a tablet or phone, you have a lot more options (and a bigger screen to see more people) when you host from a laptop or desktop computer. You should also invest in a high-resolution webcam and external USB microphone. So you and your participants get the best sound, use earphones or headphones or maybe even a headset with a built-in microphone.

- **Go with a wired connection.** As you've sometimes experienced, wireless Wi-Fi connections can sometimes be a little flakey. You can't afford a flakey connection during an important virtual event, so connect your computer to your router via Ethernet. A wired connection is both faster and more stable than a wireless one.

- **Test *everything*.** When everything's on the line, don't leave anything to chance. Test every part of the process beforehand—cameras, microphones, Internet connections, even the side apps you might be sharing during the event. Make sure everything works as promised.

- **Be professional.** Don't try to host a big-time video conference from your kitchen or bedroom. Set up in an isolated room with a door, kick out the kids and pets, and use quality external lighting. You also need to dress professionally; ditch the sweatshirt for a suit and tie or nice blouse so that you look like the host.

- **Recruit a team.** Big professional events are not one-person affairs. You need to build a team to help you with all aspects of the event, from cohosting to moderating breakout rooms. (Being able to use cohosts is another advantage of the paid Zoom versions.) Use a cohost to relieve you when necessary, provide another face onscreen, admit and welcome attendees, moderate text chat and Q&A, and even kick out disruptive attendees, if there are any. For longer events, you may even have additional presenters or panelists.

- **Start—and end—on time.** Don't accept time creep. Start promptly, allow the necessary breaks in long sessions, and end exactly when promised.

- **Email your invitations well in advance.** Give your attendees plenty of time to put your event on their schedules. Include detailed information about what they should expect, as well as what they need to prepare.

- **Create a secure meeting.** Make your meeting available only for invitees and require a password. Park all arriving attendees in the waiting room and cull out any who didn't receive a formal invitation.

- **Mute everybody's sound—and maybe turn off their cameras.** A large virtual conference or webinar is not a place for casual conversation. Mute everyone's mics when they arrive and only unmute them when you solicit participation. (That's if you allow questions, of course.) You may also want to consider turning off everyone's cameras, if you think all those individual thumbnails will be a distraction.

- **Use other media.** A big professional event is seldom just one person talking in front of a camera. Use the screensharing feature to share videos, PowerPoint presentations, whiteboards, and more. Make it a true multimedia event.

- **Record it—and share it.** Zoom lets you record large events to the cloud for future viewing. Share the URL for the recorded event with attendees after the fact so they can review it at their leisure—or share it with their friends.

Finally, you should seek feedback after any big event. Zoom allows you to conduct post-event surveys to ask attendees what they think. This is a good way to find out what went well and what didn't, so you can put on an even better event next time.

Other Livestreaming Options

Video chat is not the only way to conduct a live webinar. Other online platforms, including Facebook Live and YouTube, offer livestreaming of presentations and events.

>>>Go Further
ZOOM FOR BUSINESS

The consumer (free) version of Zoom is fine for smaller events, but if you're hosting a really large conference or seminar, subscribing to a Zoom business plan is the better way to go. The Zoom Business plan ($199.90 per year), for example, lets you host meetings with up to 300 participants, complete with breakout rooms for up to 50 smaller concurrent sessions. For an additional $600 per year (minimum), the Large Meetings add-on lets you host meetings with 500 to 1,000 interactive participants.

If you do a lot of large webinars, the Zoom Video Webinar add-on (in addition to a normal Zoom business plan) lets you have up to 100 interactive panelists, polling, performance reporting, promotional tools, pre- and post-webinar reminder emails, post-event surveys, and livestreaming to Facebook Live, YouTube, and other platforms. It's a bit pricey, though, running from $3,400 per year (for 1,000 attendees) to $64,900 per year (for 10,000 attendees).

In this chapter, you learn how to make your video chats more private and safe.

Staying Safe While Video Chatting

It seems like everybody is video chatting today, but how safe is it? Can hackers intercept your video chats, or can big companies store and sell them for a profit?

The reality is that video chatting is mostly safe for most people in most circumstances. There are some potential security and privacy issues, however, of which you should be aware.

Learning About Worrisome Privacy and Security Issues

How safe are your video chats?

Let's start with the bad news first. No video chat platform today is 100% secure 100% of the time. That means your private chats may not always stay private.

Now to the good news. Most video chats are safe enough for most people. Plus, you can take a few simple steps to improve your privacy and security (which we'll discuss in the "Making Your Video Chats More Private and Secure" section, later in this chapter).

Let's begin this discussion by examining some of the more common worries that people have about video chat privacy and security.

>>>*Go Further*
END-TO-END ENCRYPTION

Encryption is a security measure that scrambles data so that only those with the decryption key can unscramble it. In terms of video chat, standard encryption encrypts chats only between your device and the chat platform's server; the chat could still be seen by the chat company or anyone accessing their servers.

End-to-end encryption is an even more secure technology that encrypts data on each participant's device and only decrypts it when it's been received on the other person's device. With end-to-end encryption, anyone intercepting a transmission mid-stream sees only a scrambled signal, which makes it the preferred technology for video and audio chats.

End-to-end encryption also ensures that chats stay encrypted on the chat platform's servers. That means the chat company can't see your chats, nor can anyone else (such as law enforcement or hackers) accessing the chat servers.

For these reasons, end-to-end encryption is the most secure technology out there when it comes to securing video chats. While all consumer video chat platforms offer some form of encryption, only FaceTime, Google Duo, and WhatsApp offer full end-to-end encryption.

Are Companies Spying on Your Chats?

One of the biggest fears people have is that their video chat platforms are secretly listening in on or watching their chats. Can Apple, Facebook, Google, Microsoft, or Zoom spy on your video chats?

Technically, any company *not* using end-to-end encryption could view your video chats and other data. End-to-end encryption keeps your chats private from one end of the conversation to the other. Without end-to-end encryption, there is some point in the chat chain that your chats are unencrypted and viewable.

Of the video chat platforms discussed in this book, only Apple FaceTime, Google Duo, and WhatsApp employ end-to-end encryption. That means that if you use any other platform—Facebook Messenger, Google Meet, Skype, Microsoft Teams, or the free version of Zoom—the companies could spy on your chats.

The good news is that even though they can spy on you, these companies probably don't. Honestly, and don't take this as an insult, unless you're an international spy, famous politician, celebrity, or nuclear scientist, you probably don't have anything of interest to spy on. There are just too many video chats taking place every day for any entity to try to spy on all of them.

It's more likely that, instead of literally spying on your chats, your video chat company tracks your activity while you're using its service. The company might not know what you're doing or saying in your chats, but it could know who you're chatting with and for how long, as well as your location, the type of device you're using, your operating system, and other technical details. That's a little less disturbing but still what some might call an invasion of privacy. It is, however, something disclosed to you and allowed when you agree to a given company's terms of service when you first sign up, which most of us typically do without reading the fine print.

This tracking is actually quite common on all types of websites, not just chat platforms. Many Internet companies track your behavior online and then either sell that information to other companies or use it to target advertising to you on their websites or platforms. That's why when you shop for a lamp one day, lamp advertisements keep popping up for weeks. This is how companies can offer their services at no charge to you. (Facebook and Google generate the majority of their revenues from selling ads and information to other companies.)

Tracking at Work

This type of tracking is also an issue in larger businesses. If you're video chatting with someone at a big business or you're at work while you're chatting, it's possible that the company's IT staff is tracking your chat activity.

Given that location and technical tracking is pretty much part and parcel of using the Internet these days, there's not much you can do to block companies from tracking your chat activities. If you absolutely, positively don't want anyone tracking your video chats, your only recourse is to refrain from participating in video chats.

Is the Government Spying on Your Chats?

Just as the company that hosts your chat platform can spy on any unencrypted chats, so can law enforcement and government agencies—presumably, with a warrant. In fact, the government is on the record as being opposed to end-to-end encryption because they can't break in to view data or chats in transit.

Why would the government want to spy on you? Well, it probably doesn't want to spy on you personally, unless you're involved in some sort of illegal activity. Government and law enforcement agencies want to be able to tap in to online conversations the same way they tap into traditional telephone conversations to capture illegal activity and, in the case of the feds, track down terrorists. Any video chat platform that does not use end-to-end encryption can theoretically turn over its stored chat sessions to the government if requested.

Foreign Spies

There are also reported instances of intelligence agents from China, Russia, and other foreign countries actively spying on various video chat platforms. Most of these activities involve spying on large U.S. companies and government agencies to obtain confidential information. Zoom, in particular, has been the subject of many of these cyber intrusions, due to both its popularity with U.S. businesses and its (at least perceived) weak cybersecurity measures.

Are Hackers Spying on Your Chats?

Who else can spy on your video chats? What about hackers and other malicious actors?

While it's unlikely that a video chat company would willingly turn over your stored chats to a criminal organization, that criminal organization could illegally hack into the company's servers and abscond with all the chats (and other data) stored there. A malicious actor could even block access to all of a company's data unless the company agreed to pay a ransom. (This is called a ransomware attack.) Hackers can even take stolen data and make sensitive or embarrassing chats public.

The hacking risk is reduced if a chat platform uses end-to-end encryption because the stored chats would be encrypted. Still, any stored data is at risk to criminal hacking.

For that matter, hackers can break into the chat chain at any point to intercept your chat sessions. Probably the most vulnerable point is your home Wi-Fi network or the Wi-Fi networks of other chat participants. You can reduce this risk by enabling Wi-Fi security on your wireless router or gateway and using a very strong password to deter at least casual hackers.

Chatting via a public Wi-Fi hotspot carries similar security risks. Even if a chat is end-to-end encrypted, it could still be intercepted when you connect to a public network. This makes video chatting at your local coffee shop riskier than chatting at home.

Are Your Chat Partners Sharing Your Chats?

The most significant security risks are those people with whom you chat. That's right, most leaked chats come from other chatters who record their chats and make them public.

You may not be aware of this, but there are numerous apps and tools available that enable malicious actors to record entire chat sessions surreptitiously, video and all. There are also ways to record just the audio from a chat session, as well as capture static screenshots of a chat session.

If someone on your chat has bad intentions, or if you have a falling out with someone, that person could share otherwise private conversations. You may trust the person or people you're chatting with, but is that trust justified?

It's possible, for example, that the person you're casually chatting with about some upcoming business project is actually in cahoots with the competition. Or maybe that person quits or gets fired in the future and decides to take those chat recordings to his new employer.

There's also the issue of "intimate interception." This happens when a close friend or significant other inadvertently or purposefully shares something from one of your chats, either via word of mouth or via recording or screenshot. You may think you're talking in confidence, but the other person doesn't keep your chat private.

This sometimes happens to people who are long-distance dating, or who just want to stay close when one person is traveling. You can use video chat to hold what we'll call intimate conversations, but what happens if you break up with that person? Someone you've been intimate with via video chat could record those chats and share them with others or via social media. That could be embarrassing.

In some states, recording private chats without consent is illegal, but that might not stop others from doing it. Your only protection from this kind of intimate interception is to not do anything in video chats that you don't want made public.

Privacy and Security Issues with Specific Chat Platforms

In addition to the general issues that face all video chat users, some individual platforms have experienced specific privacy and security issues.

Apple FaceTime

Apple's video chat platform is one of the most secure because it uses end-to-end encryption. Apple also doesn't store information about individual chat users.

FaceTime has had some security issues. For example, in 2019, security experts discovered a bug that let Group FaceTime callers listen in on other users' audio right before or after the call. Apple quickly fixed that bug and has been pretty good about addressing other security concerns.

Facebook Messenger

Facebook Messenger is not as secure as some other video chat platforms because it doesn't use end-to-end encryption. It's also experienced some security issues, such as the bug found in late 2020 that allowed hackers to place

Messenger audio calls without the caller's knowledge. Facebook quickly fixed that bug but remains less secure than some competitors.

Like most tech companies, Facebook makes a lot of money from tracking user information and using that info to sell ads to advertisers, typically on the Facebook website. Facebook has also courted controversy by allowing third-party apps to share users' personal data, although the company has since restricted this access and enacted more transparent privacy policies.

Google Duo and Meet

Google Duo uses end-to-end encryption, which makes it among the most secure platforms currently available. Google Meet, however, only uses standard (not end-to-end) encryption, so it's less secure.

Google, like most tech companies, tracks user information and uses it to sell ad space to advertisers. (Google makes most of its money from selling ads.) This goes across all Google products, including Google search and video chat.

Microsoft Teams

Because video chat is just one part of the Microsoft Teams platform, you have to look at the security of Teams as a whole—and there are issues. The chief issue is how Teams data, including video chats, are stored—both on clients' servers and in the cloud by Microsoft. In addition, Microsoft routinely collects user data for advertising purposes.

Microsoft has also been victim to numerous security breaches. For example, in late 2019, the company's customer support database was hacked, exposing sensitive customer information. Teams experienced a similar breach a few months later in 2020, which could have let hackers hijack Teams servers.

In addition, Microsoft Teams does not yet offer end-to-end encryption. Its standard encryption is pretty good, but not as secure as true end-to-end encryption.

Skype

Like Microsoft Teams, Skype is subject to Microsoft's collection of user data for advertising purposes. It also doesn't use end-to-end encryption.

A recent scandal developed over Microsoft's use of human observers to listen in on random Skype conversations to help improve its services. The company has since moved the listening service to "secure facilities," but it still listens in. This is not ideal.

WhatsApp

WhatsApp is one of the safer video chat platforms. All WhatsApp communications employ end-to-end encryption for the highest level of security.

Unfortunately, because WhatsApp is owned by Facebook, it is subject to user data collection by the parent company. Facebook collects this user data to help it sell more targeted advertising.

Zoom

Over the past year or so, Zoom has been plagued with a variety of security and privacy issues. The most notable issue is that of Zoombombing, where unauthorized users broke into private video meetings and caused all sorts of havoc. In addition, Zoom's prior privacy policies pretty much gave the company carte blanche to use user data however it wanted.

After considerable negative feedback, however, the company changed its privacy policy and enacted some significant security changes.

To combat Zoombombing, Zoom enabled waiting rooms and default passwords for all meetings. It offers end-to-end encryption to paid users but not to free users—although the company says end-to-end encryption is coming to all users sometime in the future. The company has beefed up its security staff, acquired an identity management company, and enacted regular security updates to its platform.

Making Your Video Chats More Private and Secure

Knowing the inherent security and privacy issues, how can you make your video chats more private and secure? Here are a few simple steps you can take, with a special focus on the popular Zoom platform.

Don't Publicize Chat Invitations

During the early days of the COVID-19 crisis, many people and institutions fell victim to Zoombombing, where an uninvited person drops into a video chat and somehow disrupts the meeting. The situation became so severe that many schools dropped Zoom from their distance learning until the issue was addressed.

Zoombombing—which can happen on any video chat platform—occurs when an invitation to a private video chat goes public. For this reason, you don't want to broadcast your video chats beyond the people to whom you send invitations. Don't publicize your chats on social media or anywhere they might be seen by strangers. Keep your invitations private—and stress the same to the people you invite.

Use a Unique Meeting ID

You can avoid uninvited guests in Zoom by using unique meeting IDs instead of your own personal ID. If you use the same ID for multiple meetings, previous attendees (or people with the previous ID number) can attend future meetings, even if they're not explicitly invited.

In Zoom, all you have to do is select the unique meeting ID option when creating a new meeting. This way, every meeting will have a unique ID and can't be Zoombombed by people from other meetings.

Use a Strong Password

The other good way to block uninvited guests is to require a password to enter a video meeting. If you're using Zoom, the platform suggests a unique password; if you're manually creating your own password, make sure it's long and strong so no one can guess it.

Enable the Waiting Room

Another good security procedure offered by Facebook Messenger Rooms, Microsoft Teams, and Zoom is the waiting room or lobby that visitors must enter before they join a meeting. When you enable the waiting room feature, you have the opportunity to review and approve every participant before you admit that person to the chat. If you see people you didn't invite or don't recognize their names, have them identify themselves and, if you don't know them, just don't let them in.

Lock Your Meetings Once They Start

Once a video meeting starts and all attendees have entered, you can use the platform's "lock" feature to lock the meeting. (To do this in Zoom, open the Participants pane, click More, and then click Lock Meeting.) When a meeting is locked, no one else can enter, thus preventing uninvited guests. If an attendee leaves and intends to reenter, or if participants will be coming in later, you need to remember to unlock the meeting.

Keep Your Chat Apps Updated

Whatever chat platform you use, it's important that you update the chat apps on a regular basis. The chat platforms periodically issue app updates to add new features, fix bugs, and, in some cases, plug recently discovered vulnerabilities that hackers can take advantage of. When prompted to update a chat app, do it to keep the hackers at bay.

Use Your Web Browser Instead of the App

A safer approach is to chat via your device's web browser, if that option is available, instead of using the dedicated chat app. This is an especially good idea with Zoom, which pushes out security updates to its browser version faster than it does to its apps. In any case, most web browsers have security features that protect your system from malware that might infect a given web page. Using the browser version of a platform probably isn't a good idea on smartphones because the interface isn't optimized for smaller screens.

Zoom via the Web

Here's how to join a Zoom meeting in your computer's web browser rather than through Zoom's desktop app. When you click the meeting link in an email invitation, you open a new tab in your web browser. Instead of clicking the link to launch or install the Zoom desktop software, look for a link (typically in very small type) to "join from your browser." Click this link, and you'll join the meeting directly from your web browser instead of the Zoom desktop app.

Watch What You Screen Share

When it comes to protecting your individual privacy, be careful about what you share on your screen. You don't want to accidentally show an email with your address or credit card information on it, a spreadsheet with your personal budget, or an inappropriate video you may have been watching. Before the meeting starts, you may want to close all documents and web pages except the content you want to share.

Keep Private Information Out of the Background

You need to be aware of whatever might be captured by your camera during a video chat. Check what's behind you and what's on your physical desk to make sure the camera doesn't show any private or confidential information. Clear all the bills and private papers from view, as well as any personal photos you really don't want to share. Look at your live thumbnail to make sure there's nothing showing that you don't want others to see.

Don't Say or Show Anything You Don't Want Made Public

Finally, know that when it comes to the Internet, nothing is truly private. Anything shown or said in a video chat can be recorded or intercepted or just paraphrased by another participant. You may think you're chatting in confidence, but that confidence may not be warranted.

In other words, don't say or show anything in a video chat that you absolutely, positively don't want others to hear or see. Watch what you're sharing because you never know where it might turn up in the future.

Avoiding Screen Fatigue and Eye Strain

Sitting in front of a screen for long periods of time isn't good for you, either physically or mentally. During the COVID-19 crisis, some experts described what they called "Zoom fatigue," which is that overall feeling of tiredness when you have too many virtual meetings in a day. This fatigue is real—although you can do much to combat it.

Why do you feel tired after a long video chat or series of video chats? It's because you're sitting still without moving. You're emotionally drained. Your eyes are strained. Then there's muscle fatigue: When you sit for an extended period of time, your hips and knees are fixed in a 90-degree position. This causes your muscles to get tight and results in the stiffness you feel when you finally get up and walk around. In addition, your arms, neck, and head get stiff because you don't move them when you're looking at the screen.

To combat eye strain, check your lighting. The combination of a bright screen in a darkened room can hurt your eyes, as can a light that's too bright shining in your face. Adjust your lighting so there's not too great a contrast between the screen and the rest of the room.

To further avoid eye strain, experts recommend following what they call the "20-20-20" rule. Every 20 minutes, look at something 20 feet away for 20 seconds. That should help.

(By the way, some doctors recommend blue-light blocking glasses that block out allegedly harmful blue light from your device's display. There's not a lot of research on this, however, and the American Academy of Ophthalmology doesn't recommend them. If you do use them, know that blue-light glasses alone won't solve all your eye-strain issues.)

You can fight muscle fatigue by following some simple ergonomic advice. Make sure your screen is at eye level, so you don't have to crane your neck downward. If you're using a computer, adjust your keyboard so your shoulders are relaxed and your elbows bent. Position the height of your chair so that both your feet are touching the floor.

You also need to take some physical breaks. Don't schedule back-to-back-to-back video meetings; put a five- or ten-minute buffer in-between meetings so you can get up and stretch, walk around a little, and look at something other than your monitor.

Finally, you need to take care of your mental health as well as your physical health. Don't feel obligated to participate in every video chat to which you're invited. Too much video chatting isn't good for you; you can't let video chats take over your personal life. Set boundaries for the time you spend online, and stick to them. When it comes to video chatting, it may be okay to say no.

Glossary

Amazon Echo Show   Amazon's smart display that can be used for video chat.

Android   Google's operating system for smartphones.

backlighting   When lighting is placed behind a subject, often placing the person's face in darkness.

BlueJeans   An enterprise-oriented video conferencing platform.

earbuds   A type of small listening device that fits inside each ear.

encryption   A technique for scrambling data or communications so that only people with the designated key can decode it.

end-to-end encryption   When encryption is applied at all stages of the communications process, including the host servers.

Ethernet   The cabling used to physically connect devices in a network.

Facebook Messenger   Facebook's platform for video chat.

Facebook Portal   Facebook's smart display designed especially for video chat using Facebook Messenger.

Facebook Portal TV   A version of Facebook Portal with a display; it connects to any TV for video chatting.

FaceTime   Apple's platform for video chat.

gallery view   On some group video chat platforms, a view that displays a large number of participants in individual tiles or panes.

Google Duo   One of Google's platforms for video chat, designed for consumer use.

Google Meet   Another one of Google's platforms for video chat, designed for group calls and business use.

Google Nest Hub Max   Google's smart display that can be used for video chat using Google Duo or Google Meet.

GoToMeeting   An enterprise-oriented video conferencing platform.

green screen   A video technique that uses a green background behind the subject; the green color is digitally removed and replaced with a virtual background.

Group FaceTime   A version of Apple FaceTime designed for group video chats.

group video chat   A video chat with more than two participants.

headphones   A type of larger listening device worn on or over one's ears.

headset   A type of listening device that also has a built-in microphone.

instant meeting   A video chat that starts immediately (not scheduled in advance).

Internet service provider   See *ISP.*

intimate interception   When one of the participants in a private video chat records or takes screenshots of intimate activities and then shares them publicly or with others.

iOS   Apple's operating system for smartphones, used in the company's iPhones.

iPadOS   Apple's operating system for tablets, similar to the iOS operating system, used in the company's iPads.

ISP   Short for *Internet service provider*, a company that delivers Internet service to homes and businesses.

live streaming   The transmission of a video event or conference over the Internet in real time.

Memoji   An animated avatar that displays instead of your face onscreen but tracks all your facial movements in real time.

Messenger Rooms   Facebook's group video chat platform.

Microsoft Teams   Microsoft's collaboration platform with a component for group video chat.

one-on-one video chat   Video chat between just two participants.

pixel   Short for "picture element," a single point on a television or computer display.

resolution   The number of pixels that compose the picture on a television or computer display. The higher the resolution, the sharper the picture.

ring light   A type of LED lighting in the shape of a ring or circle.

router   A device that distributes a network signal to multiple devices.

screen sharing   The ability to share the contents of a person's screen or specific window or app with other participants of a video chat.

Skype   Microsoft's platform for video chat targeted at home users.

smart display   A variation of the smart speaker device (typified by Amazon's Echo devices) that adds a display so that the device can be used for video chat.

speaker view   On some group video chat platforms, a view that displays a large image of the person who's currently speaking and other participants in smaller live thumbnails.

Story Time   In Facebook Messenger, a feature that enables the reader to be digitally placed "within" the story onscreen.

streaming video   Video content that is transmitted over the Internet for playback in real time.

tripod   A three-legged stand, typically used to hold cameras and smartphones.

USB   Short for *universal serial bus*, a common connector used on computers and other electronic devices.

video calling   See *video chat*.

video chat   A face-to-face conversation between two or more people conducted in real time over the Internet.

video chat platform   A service that provides video chat services to its users. The most popular video chat platforms among consumers today are Apple FaceTime, Facebook Messenger, Google Duo, Google Meet, Microsoft Teams, Skype, WhatsApp, and Zoom.

video conferencing   See *video chat*.

video meeting   See *video chat*.

virtual background   An image digitally inserted behind the speaker in a video call to replace the normal physical background.

virtual event   A large meeting, either personal or professional, conducted over video chat.

waiting room   In Zoom, a virtual room where participants in a video chat are temporarily placed before being admitted to the chat.

webcam   A device, typically connected to a desktop computer, that includes a camera and microphone, used for video chat and other purposes.

Webex   An enterprise-oriented video conferencing service from Cisco.

Webinar   A web-based seminar conducted via video chat.

WhatsApp   A video chat platform from Facebook designed for smartphone use.

whiteboard   In video chats, a screen or page where participants can write or draw in real time.

Wi-Fi   A networking technology for transmitting data wirelessly.

Wickr   An enterprise-oriented video communications platform.

Zoom   The leading video chat platform today.

Zoombombing   The act of intruding on a Zoom meeting by an uninvited person.

Index

Answers to Your Technology Questions

The My...For Seniors Series is a collection of how-to guide books from AARP and Que that respect your smarts without assuming you are a techie. Each book in the series features:

- Large, full-color photos
- Step-by-step instructions
- Helpful tips and tricks
- Troubleshooting help

For more information about these titles,
and for more specialized titles, visit
informit.com/que

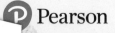

the trusted technology learning source